THE LIFE OF

King Henry the Fifth

A BLAISDELL BOOK
IN THE HUMANITIES

EDITED BY
George Lyman Kittredge

Revised by Irving Ribner

THE LIFE OF

William Shakespeare

King Henry
the Fifth

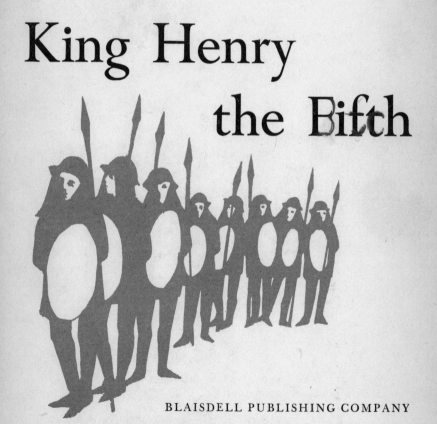

BLAISDELL PUBLISHING COMPANY

A Division of Ginn and Company

WALTHAM, MASSACHUSETTS · TORONTO · LONDON

PREFACE

The New Kittredge Shakespeares

The publication of George Lyman Kittredge's *Complete Works of Shakespeare* in 1936 was a landmark in Shakespeare scholarship. The teacher who for almost half a century had dominated and shaped the direction of Shakespearean study in America produced what was recognized widely as the finest edition of Shakespeare up to his time. In the preface to this edition Kittredge indicated his editorial principles; these allowed a paramount authority to the Folio of 1623 and countenanced few departures from it while, at the same time, refusing to "canonize the heedless type-setters of the Elizabethan printing house." Kittredge's work was marked by a judicious conservatism and a common sense rarely found in equal measure in earlier editors of Shakespeare. In the thirty-odd years which have gone by since the appearance of this monumental volume, however, considerable advances have been made in the establishment of Shakespeare's text, and our body of knowledge about the dates, sources, and general historical background of Shakespeare's plays has vastly increased. The present revision is designed to apply this new knowledge to Kittredge's work so that it may have as much value to the student and general reader of today as it had to those of thirty years ago.

Before his death Kittredge had issued, in addition to *The Complete Works,* separate editions of sixteen of the plays, each copiously annotated. Some of the notes were unusually elaborate, but they interpreted Shakespeare's language with a fullness and precision attained by few other commentators, for Kittredge had few equals in his intimate knowledge of Elizabethan English. In freshly annotating the plays I have, accordingly, tried to use

v

Kittredge's own notes as fully as space would permit. Where I have repeated his distinctive language or recorded his characteristic critical opinions, I have followed the note with the symbol [κ]; where Kittredge's definition of a term can be found in essentially the same words in other editions, I have not used the identifying symbol. Every annotator draws upon the full body of the notes of earlier editors, and to give credit for every note is impossible. Notes have been placed at page bottoms.

The brief introductions which Kittredge wrote for the plays have been replaced by new ones, for what seemed like indisputable fact some thirty years ago often appears today to be much more uncertain, and many new issues of which Kittredge was not aware have been raised in recent criticism. The new introductions seek to present what are now generally agreed to be basic facts about the plays and to give some indications of the directions which modern criticism has taken, although specific analyses of individual plays are avoided.

Such great authority attaches to Kittredge's text that it has not frequently — and never lightly — been departed from. Where changes have been made, they have usually involved the restoration of copy-text readings now generally accepted in place of the emendations of eighteenth- and nineteenth-century editors of which Kittredge, in spite of his extraordinary conservatism in this regard, sometimes too easily approved. Only rarely has an emendation been adopted in the present revision which was not also adopted by Kittredge. All departures from the copy-texts are indicated in the notes, emendations followed by the names of the editors by whom they were first proposed. Wherever Kittredge's text has been departed from for any reason, his reading is given in the notes. Modern spelling has in a few instances been substituted for Elizabethan forms which are mere spelling variations but which Kittredge nevertheless retained. His punctuation has not been altered except in a few very rare instances.

The system of recording elisions and contractions which Kittredge explained in his introduction to *The Complete Works* has been retained, as has his method of preserving to the fullest the copy-text stage directions, with all additions to them enclosed within square brackets. Although modern editors recognize the vagueness of the place settings of Elizabethan plays and are reluctant to include the place designations so favoured by eighteenth- and nineteenth-century editors, much historical interest nevertheless attaches to these, and Kittredge's place designations accordingly have been retained between square brackets. Kittredge's attempt to retain the line numbering of the Globe text, which resulted in considerable irregularity in prose passages, has been abandoned, and the lines of each play have been freshly numbered. Kittredge's act and scene divisions have been retained, as has his practice of surrounding by square brackets those divisions which are not in the copy-texts.

The plan of *The New Kittredge Shakespeares* is a comprehensive one. They will include a new edition of *The Complete Works* and individual editions of each of the plays, the sonnets, and the poems. A comprehensive introduction to Shakespeare's life, times, and theatrical milieu will be published both as a separate volume and as an introduction to *The Complete Works*.

IRVING RIBNER

INTRODUCTION

The Life of King Henry the Fifth

◇◇◇◇◇
◇◇◇◇◇
◇◇◇◇◇ *Henry V* is the final unit in the tetralogy which begins with *Richard II* and includes the two parts of *Henry IV*, for in this climactic play the hero-king has emerged, and we are permitted to view him as the suppressor of rebellion at home and the victorious conqueror abroad. Shakespeare calls him "the mirror of all Christian kings," one who may serve as a model of what a king should be, a matter of particular concern to Englishmen at the very end of the sixteenth century, with an aged and childless queen upon the throne and the identity of her successor still very much in doubt. That Henry is a model of kingship, however, does not mean that he is a model for mankind in general to emulate, for a basic theme of Shakespeare's Lancastrian plays is the difference between kings and other men. Prince Hal, in the two parts of *Henry IV*, while he learned the civil and the military virtues, was forced also to learn how to divorce himself from the ordinary feelings of humanity, the foibles, weaknesses, and natural affections which are very much a part of mankind. It is for this reason that he has seemed to some critics to be cold and even Machiavellian.

Henry V is an intensely patriotic play, with power to stir the blood even of twentieth-century Americans as fully as it must have stirred those of Tudor Englishmen. In an age which no longer sees military conquest as a primary aim of government, and which cannot conceive of absolute monarchy as an acceptable ideal of rule, the reader in his study is often tempted to find in this play his own social prejudices and to discover unadmirable qualities in the soldier-king which rarely occur to a theatre audience caught up in the heroic action and enthralled by Shakespeare's poetry of adulation. *Henry V* is thus a play which it is especially important that we view in proper historical perspective.

COMPOSITION AND PUBLICATION

The date of *Henry V* is fixed with unusual exactness by the reference to the Irish campaign of the Earl of Essex in lines 30–4 of the Chorus to Act V. Essex left London on March 27, 1599, reached Dublin in April, and, returning from a campaign which was a complete fiasco, arrived at London on September 28 of the same year. The play must then have been written well before Essex's return to London, for it was known considerably before September that the Irish campaign was a failure. *Henry V* was probably being staged in London in the summer of 1599.

On August 4, 1600, *Henry V* was entered in the Stationers' Register, along with *As You Like It, Much Ado About Nothing,* and Ben Jonson's *Every Man in His Humour,* all four plays marked "to be staied." This was apparently an attempt to prevent the unauthorized publication of what must have been extremely popular plays. That it was unsuccessful in so far as *Henry V* was concerned, we may gather from an entry in the Register on August 14, which indicates that the play had already been printed and which formally gives the copyright to Thomas Pavier. The edition in question was a quarto (Q^1) printed in 1600 by Thomas Creede for Thomas Millington and John Busby. It is a shortened and extremely corrupt text, a "bad quarto," derived almost certainly by memorial reconstruction, probably of a version of the play which had already been abbreviated for performance in the provinces. The choruses are missing, as are three whole scenes. This corrupt text served as the basis for a second quarto (Q^2) printed by Thomas Creede for Thomas Pavier in 1602, and for a third quarto (Q^3) printed by William Jaggard for Thomas Pavier in 1619 but bearing a false title page of 1608. For their copy the editors of the folio of 1623 (F^1) apparently had access to Shakespeare's own manuscript of the play (foul papers), and they produced a text which is generally a very good one and which accordingly forms the basis of the present edition. It contains act headings which seem almost certainly to have been inserted in the printing house. The act and scene divisions of the present edition follow those of the Globe text.

THE HERO-KING

To Shakespeare's contemporaries, looking back beyond the bitter years of the Wars of the Roses, Henry V was among the greatest of English kings, a man who for a brief period, aided both by fortune and divine grace, had arrested a long process of decay which had begun with the deposition of Richard II, and had achieved the last great victory over France upon which Tudor Englishmen could look back with pride, the glorious field of Agincourt. After his death chaos and disorder had returned, only to be lifted by the coming of the Tudors in 1485. This was the view which came down to Shakespeare in his principal source, Raphael Holinshed's *Chronicles of England, Scotland and Ireland* (1587), and it could be found also in Edward Hall's *Union of the Two Noble and Illustre Families of Lancaster and York* (1548), which Holinshed used as his own source, and which Shakespeare certainly consulted as well. Holinshed, in fact, is following Hall very closely when he describes his pattern of kingly excellence:

> This Henry was a king, of life without spot, a prince whom all men loved, and of none disdained, a captain against whom fortune never frowned, nor mischance once spurned, whose people him so severe a justicer both loved and obeyed (and so humane withal) that he left no offence unpunished, nor friendship unrewarded; a terror to rebels, and suppressor of sedition, his virtues notable, his qualities most praise-worthy. So staid of mind and countenance beside, that never jolly or triumphant for victory, nor sad or damped for loss or misfortune. For bountifulness and liberality, no man more free, gentle, and frank, in bestowing rewards to all persons, according to their deserts: for his saying was, that he never desired money to keep, but to give and spend.
>
> . . . Known be it therefore, of person and form was this prince rightly representing his heroical affects, of stature and proportion tall and manly, rather lean than gross, somewhat long necked and black haired, of countenance amiable, eloquent and grave was his speech, and of great grace and power to persuade: for conclusion, a majesty was he that both lived and died a pattern in princehood,

a lodestar in honour, and mirror of magnificence: the more highly exalted in his life, the more deeply lamented at his death, and famous to the world always.

That Shakespeare's King Henry was viewed in these terms by his contemporary audience there can be little doubt. Beginning perhaps with Samuel Johnson in the eighteenth century, however, there has been a critical tendency which would denigrate the character of the King, to view him as the amoral (if not immoral) politician, who invades France for reasons of political expedience, who is brutal in battle, as witness his order for the slaying of the prisoners (IV.vi.37), who is callous in his condemnation of the conspirators (II.ii), and whose religious piety is mere superstition when it is not outright hypocrisy. Although this view has persisted in various forms and degrees to our own day, it has probably never been stated more baldly than it was by William Hazlitt in his *Characters of Shakespeare's Plays* of 1817:

He was fond of war and low company: — we know little else of him. He was careless, dissolute, and ambitious, — idle, or doing mischief. In private he seemed to have no idea of the common decencies of life, which he subjected to a kind of regal licence; in public affairs, he seemed to have no idea of any rule of right or wrong, but brute force, glossed over with a little religious hypocrisy and archiepiscopal advice. His principles did not change with his situation and professions. His adventure on Gadshill was a prelude to the affair of Agincourt, only a bloodless one; Falstaff was a puny prompter of violence and outrage, compared with the pious and politic Archbishop of Canterbury, who gave the king *carte blanche*, in a genealogical tree of his family, to rob and murder in circles of latitude and longitude abroad — to save the possessions of the church at home. This appears in the speeches in Shakespeare, where the hidden motives that actuate princes and their advisers in war and policy are better laid open than in speeches from the throne or woolsack. Henry, because he did not know how to govern his own kingdom, determined to make war upon his neighbours. Because his own title to the crown was doubtful, he laid claim to that of France. Because he did not know how to exercise the enormous power, which had just dropped into his hands, to any one good purpose, he immediately undertook (a cheap and obvious resource of sovereignty) to do all the mischief he could.

If we attempt to view King Henry as Shakespeare's audience might have viewed him, however, the principal modern objections to his conduct tend to disappear. His claim to the throne of France could not be disputed or dismissed as political trickery by Tudor Englishmen, for they regarded their own Elizabeth as rightfully queen of France as well as England, by virtue of the same rights of King Edward III which Henry asserts. The condemnation of the rebels would hardly seem cruel to an audience which could see in that uprising the seeds of the Wars of the Roses, and the slaughter of prisoners by an outnumbered band of men incapable of guarding prisoners while defending themselves against an overwhelming force would not seem contrary to the best military practice. That Shakespeare in this play can emphasize the horrors of war at the very same time that he celebrates the glory of English heroism and victory against odds is entirely characteristic of his genius, and it does not diminish the stature of his soldier-king.

HEROIC DRAMA

While the four plays of Shakespeare's Lancastrian tetralogy form a comprehensive interrelated whole, each part is a separate entity which can stand alone, and each part called for a different kind of dramatic structure. In *Richard II* Shakespeare had forged a tragedy of rise and fall, with Richard falling and Henry Bolingbroke rising in his place, to mark the emergence of the house of Lancaster. In the two parts of *Henry IV* Shakespeare had drawn upon the well-established pattern of the morality drama to delineate the education of Prince Hal for kingship. Now in *Henry V* the celebration of a triumphant hero called for a new structure, and for this purpose Shakespeare further developed the form of heroic drama which had been most notably introduced to the English stage by Christopher Marlowe in the two parts of *Tamburlaine,* published in 1590. A heroic play concentrated all of its focus upon its single titular hero, subordinating all other characters so as to throw light upon different aspects of the one dominant personality, and exhibiting him in a series of scenes, sometimes loosely related to one another, but each designed to further augment the audience's sense of the hero's greatness.

Partly to achieve this effect of concentration upon his hero, Shakespeare greatly abridged and simplified the account of Henry V which he found in Holinshed. Historically the play covers the period from 1414 to 1420, which included two campaigns in France, the first culminating in the victory at Agincourt in 1415 and the second in the Treaty of Troyes in 1420. Shakespeare achieves dramatic intensity by concentrating all of the military events into a single campaign which includes the siege of Harfleur, the falling back to Calais and the triumph at Agincourt. This is followed immediately by the Treaty of Troyes, although the chorus to Act V does tell of the king's return to England, where the Holy Roman Emperor came to intercede with him on the part of France, an event which occurred in May 1416. Shakespeare in his choruses informs his audience of his historical omissions.

THE DEATH OF FALSTAFF

In his epilogue to *Henry IV, Part Two,* Shakespeare had promised to "continue the story, with Sir John in it." He failed to keep his promise, however, for instead of Falstaff we have in *Henry V* merely one gemlike scene (I.iii), one of the most perfect in all Shakespeare, in which the death of the fat knight is described. It has been suggested that since the part may have been played by Will Kempe and since Kempe left Shakespeare's company shortly before 1599, Shakespeare was forced to dispose of Falstaff. There is no certainty, however, that Falstaff was played by Kempe; he may just as possibly have been acted by Thomas Pope, an actor of considerable girth. Some scholars have argued that in an original version of *Henry V* Shakespeare's promise was kept and Falstaff appeared, but that because of the opposition of the Brooke family, descendants of Sir John Oldcastle, Shakespeare was forced to rewrite his play omitting Falstaff from it. This notion seems very difficult to reconcile, however, with the undisturbed continuance of the fat knight in the two parts of *Henry IV.*

It may be that Shakespeare fully intended when he wrote his 2 *Henry IV* epilogue to retain in his next play what was obviously an extremely popular stage attraction, but when he came to write *Henry V* he may have found it impossible for him to do so. In this play Falstaff could no longer have any real dramatic function. He had been rejected completely and finally, and Shakespeare could only describe his death. When Shakespeare created a Falstaff without political implications and without a morality function, in *The Merry Wives of Windsor,* the fat knight was merely a pale shadow of his original.

THE MINOR CHARACTERS

While Shakespeare's attention is always fixed upon his hero-king, *Henry V* is a play extraordinarily rich in its portraiture of English society, encompassing virtually every element of the social scale. It may have been in part to replace Falstaff as a comic butt that he built up the character of Pistol, the supreme braggart soldier of English drama. To Prince Hal's former associates he added the "humorous" Corporal Nym. It must be noted that these characters are treated more ignominiously than in the *Henry IV* plays. They are the camp followers who go to the wars for plunder and who, while they present a graphic portrait of the moral degradation of which armies are capable, serve also to point up by contrast the heroism of such warriors as Exeter and Erpingham, as well as the simple fidelity of common soldiers like Bates, Court, and Williams whose very human fears on the eve of battle help introduce the moral issues which no great poet who would treat of war can really avoid. In Gower, Macmorris, Jamy, and most notably, Fluellen, Shakespeare gives us a sense of England, Ireland, Scotland, and Wales joined together in the fellowship of battle for a common cause, but at the same time he creates distinctive personalities who are far more than national stereotypes. The French are generally subjected to derision, for it is natural for soldiers to deride the enemy. There are few scenes in the world's literature more winning than that of Princess Katherine at her English lesson.

THE LIFE OF
King Henry the Fifth

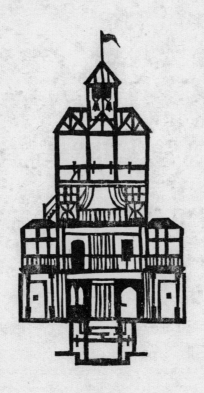

[DRAMATIS PERSONÆ.

CHORUS.

KING HENRY THE FIFTH.
DUKE OF GLOUCESTER, }
DUKE OF BEDFORD, } *brothers to the* KING.
DUKE OF EXETER, *uncle to the* KING.
DUKE OF YORK, *cousin to the* KING.
EARL OF SALISBURY.
EARL OF WESTMORELAND.
EARL OF WARWICK.
ARCHBISHOP OF CANTERBURY.
BISHOP OF ELY.
EARL OF CAMBRIDGE.
LORD SCROOP.
SIR THOMAS GREY.
SIR THOMAS ERPINGHAM, ⎫
GOWER, *an English captain,* ⎪
FLUELLEN, *a Welsh captain,* ⎬ *officers in* KING
MACMORRIS, *an Irish captain,* ⎪ HENRY'S *army.*
JAMY, *a Scottish captain,* ⎭
JOHN BATES, ⎫
ALEXANDER COURT, ⎬ *soldiers in the same.*
MICHAEL WILLIAMS, ⎭
PISTOL.
NYM.
BARDOLPH.
Boy.
A Herald.

CHARLES THE SIXTH, *King of France.*
LEWIS, *the Dauphin.*
DUKE OF BURGUNDY.
DUKE OF ORLEANS.
DUKE OF BOURBON.
DUKE OF BRETAGNE.
THE CONSTABLE OF FRANCE.
RAMBURES, ⎫
GRANDPRÉ, ⎬ *French lords.*
BEAUMONT, ⎭
GOVERNOR of *Harfleur.*
MONTJOY, *a French herald.*
Ambassadors to the KING OF ENGLAND.

ISABEL, *Queen of France.*
KATHERINE, *daughter to* CHARLES *and* ISABEL.
ALICE, *a lady attending on her.*
Hostess of the Boar's Head tavern in Eastcheap
    (*formerly* MISTRESS QUICKLY, *now married to* PISTOL).

Lords, Ladies, Officers, Soldiers, Citizens, Messengers, and Attendants.

SCENE. — *England and France.*]

Enter Prologue.

O for a <u>Muse of fire,</u> that would ascend
The <u>brightest heaven of invention,</u>
A kingdom for a stage, princes to act,
And monarchs to behold the <u>swelling</u> scene!
Then should the warlike Harry, <u>like himself,</u>   5
Assume the <u>port</u> of Mars, and at his heels
(<u>Leash'd in,</u> like hounds) should famine, sword, and fire
Crouch for employment. But pardon, <u>gentles</u> all,
The <u>flat unraised spirits</u> that <u>hath</u> dar'd
On this unworthy <u>scaffold</u> to bring forth   10
So great an object. Can this <u>cockpit</u> hold
The vasty fields of France? Or may we cram
Within this <u>wooden O</u> <u>the very casques</u>
That did affright the air at Agincourt?
O, pardon! since a crooked figure may   15
<u>Attest</u> in little place a million,
And let us, <u>ciphers to</u> this great <u>accompt,</u>
On <u>your imaginary forces</u> work.
Suppose <u>within the girdle of</u> these walls

PROLOGUE. 1 *Muse of fire* Since fire was believed to be the lightest and most etherial of the four elements, whose natural tendency it was to rise, it was generally associated with poets. 2 *brightest heaven of invention* the empyrean of Ptolemaic astronomy, to which fire in its purest form was believed to ascend. From this sphere would come such inspiration as the poet needed to write of mighty kings and battles. "Invention" refers specifically to "poetic creativity.". 4 *swelling* magnificent. 5 *like himself* acted in such a way as to resemble the king himself, in all his uniqueness and greatness. 6 *port* bearing. 7 *Leash'd in* A "leash" of hounds consisted of three dogs fastened together. 8 *gentles* gentlemen and ladies [K]. 9 *flat unraised spirits* uninspired intellects [K]. *hath* A singular verb with a plural subject is commonly used by Shakespeare (F¹; K: "have"). 10 *scaffold* stage. 11 *cockpit* The theatre was circular or octagonal, and the seats rose in tiers, so that it was not unlike the pits in which cockfights were held [K]. 13 *wooden O* wooden circle. *the very casques* even the helmets (to say nothing of the men who wore them). 15-16 *crooked figure . . . million* a mere zero, in the proper position, may increase the value of a number by a million. *Attest* stand for, signify. 17 *ciphers to* mere zeroes in comparison with. *this great accompt* (a) this great amount or total (b) this great story — account. 18 *your imaginary forces* the powers of your imagination [K]. 19 *within the girdle of* encompassed by (as by a belt).

Are now confin'd two mighty monarchies,   20
Whose <u>high-upreared and abutting fronts</u>
The perilous <u>narrow ocean</u> parts asunder.
Piece out our imperfections with your thoughts:
Into a thousand parts divide one man
And make imaginary <u>puissance</u>.   25
Think, when we talk of horses, that you see them
Printing their proud hoofs i' th' receiving earth.
For 'tis your thoughts that now must <u>deck</u> our kings,
Carry them here and there, jumping o'er times,
Turning <u>th' accomplishment of many years</u>   30
Into an hourglass; <u>for the which supply</u>,
Admit me Chorus to this history,
Who, <u>Prologue-like,</u> your humble patience pray,
Gently to hear, kindly to judge our play.   *Exit.*

---

21 *high-upreared . . . fronts* the cliffs of Dover and Calais.   22 *narrow ocean* English Channel.   25 *puissance* forces, troops. The word is sometimes trisyllabic (as here) sometimes dissyllabic [ĸ].   28 *deck* equip, dress.   30 *th' accomplishment of many years* the deeds done over a period of many years. The events of the play cover the six-year period from 1414 to 1420.   31 *for the which supply* to fill up the defects just mentioned (i.e. by describing what the players cannot act or represent) [ĸ].   33 *Prologue-like* in the guise of a Prologue, or in the manner of a Prologue — probably the former, the Prologue having a conventional costume. The gist of the whole Chorus is, then, an apology, with an appeal to the audience to use their imagination and a promise to explain or fill in what the action cannot afford. The other choruses are to much the same effect [ĸ].

[Act One]

◇◇◇

SCENE I.
[London. An antechamber in the King's *Palace.]*

Enter the two Bishops — [the Archbishop] of Canterbury *and* [the Bishop of] Ely.

CANT.   My lord, I'll tell you, that <u>self</u> bill is <u>urg'd</u>
   Which in th' eleventh year of the last king's reign
   Was like, and had indeed against us pass'd
   But that the <u>scambling</u> and unquiet time
   Did push it out of farther <u>question</u>.   5

ELY.   But how, my lord, shall we resist it now?

CANT.   It must be thought on. If it pass against us,
   We lose the better half of our possession;
   For all the <u>temporal lands</u> which men devout
   By testament have given to the Church   10
   Would they strip from us; being valu'd thus —
   As much as would maintain, to the King's honour,
   Full fifteen earls and fifteen hundred knights,
   Six thousand and two hundred good esquires,
   And, to relief of <u>lazars</u> and weak <u>age</u>,   15

I.I.   The effect of the first act is to relieve King Henry, in the minds of the audience, of any responsibility for the war that is to ensue. The clergy take all upon their consciences. We also have the most favourable exposition of the justice of his cause. And at the end of the act the Dauphin's wanton insult adds the touch of personal injury which makes the conflict interesting as the King's own war rather than as a mere matter of political aggrandizement [K]. 1 *self* same. *urg'd* proposed. 4 *scambling* turbulent, unruly. 5 *question* discussion, consideration. 9 *temporal lands* estates not actually used for worship or devotion [K]. 15 *lazars* lepers — but used rather loosely for those afflicted with other similar diseases as well [K]. *age* aged persons (abstract for concrete) [K].

3

Of indigent faint souls, past <u>corporal toil,</u>
A hundred almshouses right well supplied;
And to the coffers of the King beside,
A thousand pounds by th' year. Thus runs the bill.

ELY. This would drink deep.

CANT.   'Twould drink the cup and all.   20

ELY. But what <u>prevention</u>?

CANT. The King is full of grace and <u>fair regard</u>.

ELY. And a true lover of the holy Church.

CANT. The <u>courses of his youth</u> promis'd it not.
The breath no sooner left his father's body   25
But that his wildness, <u>mortified</u> in him,
Seem'd to die too. Yea, at that very moment
<u>Consideration</u> like an angel came
And whipp'd <u>th' offending Adam</u> out of him,
Leaving his body as a paradise   30
T'envelop and contain celestial spirits.
Never was such a sudden scholar made;
Never came reformation in a flood
With such a <u>heady currance</u> scouring faults;
Nor never <u>hydra-headed</u> wilfulness   35
So soon did lose his <u>seat</u>, and all at once,
As in this king.

ELY.   We are blessed in the change.

CANT. Hear him but reason in <u>divinity</u>,
And, all-admiring, with an inward wish

---

16 *corporal toil* physical labour.   21 *prevention* means of forestalling such action.
22 *fair regard* kindly consideration.   24 *courses of his youth* King Henry's riotous
youth had been set before Elizabethan playgoers in the First and Second Parts of
Shakespeare's HENRY IV [K].   26 *mortified* killed.   28 *Consideration* mature, sober
thoughtfulness.   29 *th' offending Adam* original sin, the hereditary sinfulness inherited from Adam. Also called "the old Adam," from the biblical phrase [K].
34 *heady currance* headstrong, impetuous current. There may be an implicit allusion to the cleansing of the Augean stables by Hercules, who accomplished this
task by sending a river through them.   35 *hydra-headed* many headed. The Hydra
of Lerna was a many-headed monster slain by Hercules.   36 *seat* power (literally,
"throne").   38 *divinity* theology.   43 *List* listen to.   44 *A fearful . . . music* (a)
a terrible battle so described that order and harmony will be revealed behind its
chaos and discord (b) a terrible battle described with moving eloquence.   45 *cause
of policy* political problem.   46 *Gordian knot* i.e. seemingly insoluble difficulty.
The expression comes from the legend of Alexander the Great, who supposedly

You would desire the King were made a prelate;   40
Hear him debate of commonwealth affairs,
You would say it hath been all in all his study;
List his discourse of war, and you shall hear
A fearful battle rend'red you in music;
Turn him to any cause of policy,   45
The Gordian knot of it he will unloose,
Familiar as his garter; that, when he speaks,
The air, a charter'd libertine, is still,
And the mute wonder lurketh in men's ears
To steal his sweet and honey'd sentences;   50
So that the art and practice part of life
Must be the mistress to this theoric;
Which is a wonder how his Grace should glean it,
Since his addiction was to courses vain,
His companies unletter'd, rude, and shallow,   55
His hours fill'd up with riots, banquets, sports;
And never noted in him any study,
Any retirement, any sequestration
From open haunts and popularity.

ELY.   The strawberry grows underneath the nettle,   60
And wholesome berries thrive and ripen best
Neighbour'd by fruit of baser quality;
And so the Prince obscur'd his contemplation
Under the veil of wildness, which (no doubt)
Grew like the summer grass, fastest by night,   65
Unseen, yet crescive in his faculty.

had cut the extremely intricate knot which bound the yoke to the shaft of the
wagon of King Gordius, thus fulfilling a prophecy that he who did so would
achieve mastery of all Asia.   48 *charter'd libertine* a licensed freeman, one permitted to go wherever he pleases.   49 *the mute . . . ears* wonder keeps men silent
and makes them listen eagerly [K].   50 *sentences* wise sayings.   51–2 *the art . . .
this theoric* Since the King never studied any of these subjects, he must have acquired his knowledge of their "theory" from experience in practical life. Yet that
does not decrease the wonder of it all, since his pursuits were not such as to give
him experience in such matters [K].   *mistress* authoress, teacher.   54 *vain* idle.
55 *rude* uncultivated.   58 *sequestration* separation.   59 *open haunts* public places,
frequented by the common people.   *popularity* association with commoners. A de-
rogatory term.   60–2 *The strawberry . . . quality* This was a common Elizabethan
notion about gardening.   63 *contemplation* philosophical frame of mind.   66
crescive growing.   *in his faculty* by its own natural power.

CANT.   It must be so; for <u>miracles are ceas'd</u>,
          And therefore we must needs admit the means
          How things are perfected.

ELY.   But, my good lord,
          How now for mitigation of this bill   70
          Urg'd by the commons? Doth his Majesty
          Incline to it, or no?

CANT.   He seems <u>indifferent</u>;
          Or rather swaying more upon our part
          Than<u> cherishing th' exhibiters against us</u>;
          For I have made an offer to his Majesty —   75
          <u>Upon</u> our spiritual Convocation,
          And in regard of causes now <u>in hand</u>,
          Which I have <u>open'd</u> to his Grace <u>at large</u>,
          As touching France — to give a greater sum
          Than ever at one time the clergy yet   80
          Did to his predecessors part withal.

ELY.   How did this offer seem receiv'd, my lord?

CANT.   With good acceptance of his Majesty;
          Save that there was not time enough to hear,
          As I perceiv'd his Grace would <u>fain</u> have done,   85
          The <u>severals</u> and <u>unhidden passages</u>
          Of his true titles to some certain dukedoms,
          And generally to the crown and <u>seat</u> of France,
          Deriv'd from Edward, his great-grandfather.

ELY.   What was th' impediment that broke this off?   90

CANT.   The French ambassador upon that instant
          Crav'd audience; and the hour I think is come
          To give him hearing. Is it four o'clock?

ELY.   It is.

67 *miracles are ceas'd* It was a Protestant doctrine that miracles had ended with
the Revelation. Natural causes must be found for all subsequent events.   72 *indifferent* impartial.   74 *cherishing . . . us* favouring those who make representa-
tions, or proposals, against us [K].   76 *Upon* as the result of.   77 *in hand* under
consideration.   78 *open'd* expounded, explained.   *at large* fully.   85 *fain* gladly.
86 *severals* details.   *unhidden passages* clear and undisputed descent (through lineal
inheritance).   88 *seat* throne.
     I.II. The dignity and seriousness of King Henry, for which the preceding scene

CANT.   Then go we in to know his embassy,   95
        Which I could with a ready guess declare
        Before the Frenchman speak a word of it.

ELY.   I'll wait upon you, and I long to hear it.   *Exeunt.*

◇◇◇◇◇◇◇◇◇◇◇◇◇◇◇◇

[SCENE II.
London. The presence chamber in the Palace.]

Enter the King, Humphrey [Duke of Gloucester], Bed-
        ford, Clarence, Warwick, Westmoreland, *and* Exeter,
        [*with* Attendants].

KING.   Where is my gracious Lord of Canterbury?

EXE.   Not here in presence.

KING.   Send for him, good uncle.

WEST.   Shall we call in th' ambassador, my liege?

KING.   Not yet, my cousin. We would be resolv'd,
        Before we hear him, of some things of weight,   5
        That task our thoughts, concerning us and France.

                    Enter two Bishops — [*the* Archbishop
                        of Canterbury *and the* Bishop of Ely].

CANT.   God and his angels guard your sacred throne
        And make you long become it!

KING.   Sure we thank you.
        My learned lord, we pray you to proceed
        And justly and religiously unfold   10

has prepared us, are emphasized the moment he begins to speak. The occasion lends
itself readily to this, and the royal "we" is used with much consistency [K].   2
presence the presence chamber, where the King gives public audiences.   3 *liege*
liege lord.   4 *my cousin* i.e. by marriage. Westmoreland had married Joan Beau-
fort, a descendant of John of Gaunt, Henry's grandfather. *be resolv'd* have our
doubts cleared up.   6 *task* trouble, occupy.   8 *become it* be an ornament to it.
10 *unfold* explain, reveal.

Why the Law Salique, that they have in France,
Or should or should not bar us in our claim.
And God forbid, my dear and faithful lord,
That you should fashion, wrest, or bow your reading,
Or nicely charge your understanding soul   15
With opening titles miscreate whose right
Suits not in native colours with the truth;
For God doth know how many, now in health,
Shall drop their blood in approbation
Of what your reverence shall incite us to.   20
Therefore take heed how you impawn our person,
How you awake our sleeping sword of war.
We charge you in the name of God, take heed;
For never two such kingdoms did contend
Without much fall of blood, whose guiltless drops   25
Are every one a woe, a sore complaint
'Gainst him whose wrongs gives edge unto the swords
That makes such waste in brief mortality.
Under this conjuration speak, my lord;
For we will hear, note, and believe in heart   30
That what you speak is in your conscience wash'd
As pure as sin with baptism.

CANT.   Then hear me, gracious sovereign, and you peers,
That owe yourselves, your lives, and services
To this imperial throne. There is no bar   35
To make against your Highness' claim to France
But this which they produce from Pharamond:
"In terram Salicam mulieres ne succedant";

---

11 *the Law Salique* the so-called Salic Law, which settled the crown of France on male heirs only [K]. It actually had little basis in law but stemmed from the election of Philip of Valois by the French nobility so as to prevent the throne's falling into the hands of a woman. It was later used to deny the claim of King Edward III to the French throne by right of his mother, Isabella.   12 *Or should* either should. 14 *reading* interpretation of the law.   15 *nicely . . . soul* be so foolish as to burden your soul (which understands the truth of the matter) with guilt. The antithesis between "nicely" and "understanding" is quite in the formal and balanced style appropriate to the serious speeches of historical drama [K].   16 *opening* setting forth. *miscreate* miscreated, unrighteously fabricated [K].   17 *in native colours* in the colours they have by nature. Such titles would have to be "coloured" by art to make them look like the truth [K].   19–20 *in approbation Of* in proving the

"No woman shall succeed in Salique land."
Which Salique land the French unjustly <u>gloze</u>   40
To be the realm of France, and Pharamond
The founder of this law and <u>female bar</u>.
Yet their own authors faithfully affirm
That the land Salique is in Germany,
Between the <u>floods</u> of Sala and of <u>Elbe</u>;   45
Where Charles the Great, having subdu'd the Saxons,
There left behind and settled certain French;
Who, holding in disdain the German women
For some <u>dishonest</u> manners of their life,
Establish'd then this law: to wit, no female   50
Should be inheritrix in Salique land;
Which Salique (as I said) 'twixt Elbe and Sala
Is at this day in Germany call'd Meisen.
Then doth it well appear the Salique Law
Was not devised for the realm of France;   55
Nor did the French possess the Salique land
Until four hundred one and twenty years
After <u>defunction</u> of King Pharamond,
<u>Idly</u> suppos'd the founder of this law,
Who died within the year of our redemption   60
Four hundred twenty-six; and Charles the Great
Subdu'd the Saxons, and did seat the French
Beyond the river Sala, in the year
Eight hundred five. Besides, their writers say,
King Pepin, which deposed Childeric,   65
Did, as <u>heir general</u>, being descended
Of Blithild, which was daughter to King Clothair,

---

justice of — i.e. by an appeal to the judgment of war [K].   21 *impawn* pledge.   27 *wrongs* F¹; K: "wrong."   28 *makes . . . mortality* causes such destruction of brief lives. *makes* F¹; K: "make."   29 *conjuration* solemn adjuration.   35 *imperial* so called as reigning over more kingdoms than one. The adjective subtly forecasts the archbishop's intention to urge the King to assert his claim to France [K].   37 *Pharamond* a legendary king of the Salian Franks. Shakespeare in this long argument follows Holinshed very closely.   40 *gloze* gloss, interpret (often with a suggestion of a forced or tricky interpretation) [K].   42 *female bar* prohibition to women.   45 *floods* rivers. *Elbe* CAPELL; F¹: "Elue," the form of the word in Hall's chronicle.   49 *dishonest* unchaste.   58 *defunction* death.   59 *Idly* foolishly, without good reason.   66 *heir general* one with the right to succeed, whether it be through male or female line.

Make claim and title to the crown of France.
Hugh Capet also — who usurp'd the crown
Of Charles the Duke of Lorraine, sole heir male   70
Of the true line and stock of Charles the Great —
To <u>find</u> his title with some <u>shows</u> of truth,
Though in pure truth it was corrupt and naught,
<u>Convey'd himself</u> <u>as heir</u> to th' Lady <u>Lingare,</u>
Daughter to <u>Charlemain</u>, who was the son   75
To Lewis the Emperor, and Lewis the son
Of Charles the Great. Also King <u>Lewis the Tenth,</u>
Who was sole heir to the usurper Capet,
Could not keep quiet in his conscience,
Wearing the crown of France, till satisfied   80
That fair Queen Isabel, his grandmother,
Was lineal of the Lady <u>Ermengare,</u>
Daughter to Charles the foresaid Duke of Lorraine;
By the which marriage the line of Charles the Great
Was reunited to the crown of France.   85
So that, as clear as is the summer's sun,
King Pepin's title and Hugh Capet's claim,
King Lewis <u>his satisfaction</u>, all appear
To hold in right and title of the female.
So do the kings of France unto this day,   90
Howbeit they would hold up this Salique Law
To bar your Highness claiming from the female,
And rather choose <u>to hide them in a net</u>
Than <u>amply</u> to <u>imbare</u> their crooked titles
Usurp'd from you and your progenitors.   95

KING.   <u>May I with right and conscience make this claim</u>?

---

72 *find* furnish, provide (F¹; Q¹, κ: "fine"). *shows* outward (though false) appearances.   74 *Convey'd himself* passed himself off as. To "convey" often means to
"steal."   *as heir* Q¹; F¹: "as th' Heire."   *Lingare* The name appears as "Lingard"
in Holinshed.   75 *Charlemain* Shakespeare here perpetuates an error both in Hall
and Holinshed. She was actually the daughter of Charles the Bald.   77 *Lewis the
Tenth* Historically, it should be Louis IX, as it is in Hall. The error is in Holinshed, which Shakespeare follows.   82 *Ermengare* It is "Ermengard" in Holinshed.
88 *his satisfaction* his having had his doubts removed.   93 *to hide them in a net*
to resort to a transparent subterfuge. A proverbial expression [κ].   94 *amply* completely.   *imbare* lay bare (WARBURTON; F¹: "imbarre"). Some editors read "unbar."
96 *May I . . . claim* After all this argument it is proper that the King should sum
up the question in this direct and simple way. It has the effect of honesty and
straightforwardness and leaves the audience with no doubt of his good faith, what-

CANT. The sin upon my head, dread sovereign!
       For in the Book of Numbers is it writ:
       When the man dies, let the inheritance
       Descend unto the daughter. Gracious lord,   100
       Stand for your own, unwind your bloody flag,
       Look back into your mighty ancestors;
       Go, my dread lord, to your great-grandsire's tomb,
       From whom you claim; invoke his warlike spirit,
       And your great-uncle's, Edward the Black Prince,   105
       Who on the French ground play'd a tragedy,
       Making defeat on the full power of France,
       Whiles his most mighty father on a hill
       Stood smiling to behold his lion's whelp
       Forage in blood of French nobility.   110
       O noble English, that could entertain
       With half their forces the full pride of France
       And let another half stand laughing by,
       All out of work and cold for action!

ELY.   Awake remembrance of these valiant dead   115
       And with your puissant arm renew their feats.
       You are their heir; you sit upon their throne;
       The blood and courage that renowned them
       Runs in your veins; and my thrice-puissant liege
       Is in the very May-morn of his youth,   120
       Ripe for exploits and mighty enterprises.

EXE.   Your brother kings and monarchs of the earth
       Do all expect that you should rouse yourself,
       As did the former lions of your blood.

ever they may think of the eloquent ecclesiastics [K].   98 *the Book of Numbers*
Cf. NUMBERS, XXVII, 8. It was customary to seek authority for modern law and practice in special Hebrew legislation in the Old Testament [K].   103 *great-grandsire's*
Edward III's. His marriage to Isabella, daughter of King Philip IV of France, was
the basis of Henry's claim.   106 *a tragedy* i.e. the Battle of Crécy in 1346, in which
the French were badly defeated.   110 *Forage in* prey upon.   112 *half their forces*
Actually, one third of the English forces had remained in reserve with King Edward III, while the remaining two thirds, under the command of Edward the
Black Prince, defeated the French.   114 *for action* for want of something to do
[K].   119 *thrice-puissant* i.e. since he carries on the strengths of Edward III, Edward the Black Prince, and his own father, King Henry IV.   120 *youth* The King
was actually twenty-seven years old at the time.

WEST.	They know your Grace hath cause and means and might; 125
	So hath your Highness. Never king of England
	Had nobles richer and more loyal subjects,
	Whose hearts have left their bodies here in England
	And lie <u>pavilion'd</u> in the fields of France.
CANT.	O, let their bodies follow, my dear liege, 130
	With <u>blood</u> and sword and fire, to win your right!
	In aid whereof we of the spiritualty
	Will raise your Highness such a mighty sum
	As never did the clergy at one time
	Bring in to any of your ancestors. 135
KING.	We must not only arm t' invade the French,
	But <u>lay down our proportions</u> to defend
	Against the Scot, who will make <u>road</u> upon us
	<u>With all advantages</u>.
CANT.	They of those <u>marches</u>, gracious sovereign, 140
	Shall be a wall sufficient to defend
	Our inland from the pilfering borderers.
KING.	We do not mean the <u>coursing snatchers</u> only,
	But fear <u>the main intendment of the Scot</u>,
	Who hath been <u>still</u> a <u>giddy</u> neighbour to us; 145
	For you shall read that my great-grandfather
	Never went with his forces into France
	But that the Scot on his <u>unfurnish'd</u> kingdom
	Came pouring like the tide into a breach,
	With ample and brim fulness of his force, 150
	<u>Galling</u> the <u>gleaned</u> land with hot <u>assays</u>,

129 *pavilion'd* encamped. In spirit, they are already at war.   131 *blood* F³; F¹: "Bloods."   136–9 *We must not . . . advantages* The King's conscientious scruples are satisfied. His caution, however, appears in what follows. The result of the whole method of presentation is to make the French War seem to have been entered upon, not upon any impulse of Henry's, but with the utmost deliberation. It is set forth almost as a holy war [K].   137 *lay down our proportions* plan our levies of troops [K].   138 *road* inroad.   139 *With all advantages* whenever he sees a good opportunity [K].   140 *marches* borders.   143 *coursing snatchers* swift-riding thieves. In the sport of "coursing" hares were pursued by greyhounds; the "snatch" was the dog's act of seizing his prey.   144 *the main . . . Scot* the purpose of the whole body of the Scottish nation [K].   145 *still* always. *giddy* fickle, untrustworthy.   148 *unfurnish'd* unprotected, without defences.   151 *Galling* worrying. To "gall" is properly to "excoriate," "knock off the skin." It is often used figuratively by Shakespeare [K].   *gleaned* already stripped of its defenders [K].   *assays* attacks.   154 *ill neighbourhood* poor behaviour of a neighbour.   155 *fear'd*

Girding with grievous siege castles and towns;
That England, being empty of defence,
Hath shook and trembled at th' ill neighbourhood.

CANT.   She hath been then more fear'd than harm'd, my liege;   155
For hear her but exampled by herself:
When all her chivalry hath been in France,
And she a mourning widow of her nobles,
She hath herself not only well defended
But taken and impounded as a stray   160
The King of Scots; whom she did send to France
To fill King Edward's fame with prisoner kings,
And make her chronicle as rich with praise
As is the ooze and bottom of the sea
With sunken wrack and sumless treasuries.   165

ELY.   But there's a saying very old and true —
    "If that you will France win,
    Then with Scotland first begin."
For once the eagle (England) being in prey,
To her unguarded nest the weasel (Scot)   170
Comes sneaking, and so sucks her princely eggs,
Playing the mouse in absence of the cat,
To tame and havoc more than she can eat.

EXE.   It follows then, the cat must stay at home.
Yet that is but a crush'd necessity,   175
Since we have locks to safeguard necessaries,
And pretty traps to catch the petty thieves.
While that the armed hand doth fight abroad,

frightened.   156 *hear her . . . by herself* listen to an example to Englishmen taken from the history of England itself. This refers to the captivity of David II [K]. King David II of Scotland was captured by the English forces at the same time that King Edward III was defeating the French at Crécy.   160 *taken . . . stray* Said contemptuously — "put into the pound," as was done with cattle found wandering out of their owner's fields [K].   161 *to France* King David was actually imprisoned in London, not sent to France.   163 *her* CAPELL; F¹: "their"; Q¹: "your."   165 *wrack* wrecked ships. *sumless* incalculable.   166 *Ely* F¹; CAPELL, K give the speech to Westmoreland on the grounds that he would have been more familiar with Scottish affairs, but this is to correct Shakespeare and to prejudge his intentions. There is no need for the emendation.   169 *in prey* absent in search of prey.   173 *tame* attame, cut into (F¹; ROWE: "tear"; K: "spoil"). *havoc* tear apart.   175 *crush'd* diminished (F¹; Q¹; K: "curst").   177 *pretty . . . petty* The jingle is of course intentional. It emphasizes the light tone of the speech and expresses contempt for the Scots [K].

Th' <u>advised</u> head defends itself at home;
For government, though high, and low, and lower,⎫   180
Put into parts, doth keep in one consent,   ⎬
<u>Congreeing</u> in a full and natural close,
Like music.

CANT.   <u>True</u>! Therefore doth heaven divide
The state of man in divers functions,
Setting endeavour in continual motion;   185
To which is fixed as an aim or <u>butt</u>
Obedience; for so work the honeybees,
Creatures that by a rule in nature teach
<u>The act of order</u> to a peopled kingdom.
They have a king, and officers of sorts,   190
Where some like magistrates <u>correct</u> at home,
Others like merchants venture trade abroad,
Others like soldiers armed <u>in</u> their stings
<u>Make boot upon</u> the summer's velvet buds,
Which pillage they with merry march bring home   195
To the tent-royal of their emperor,
Who, busied in his <u>majesty</u>, surveys
The singing masons building roofs of gold,
The <u>civil</u> citizens kneading up the honey,
The poor <u>mechanic</u> porters crowding in   200
Their heavy burdens at his narrow gate,
The <u>sad-ey'd</u> justice, with his surly hum,
Delivering o'er to <u>executors</u> pale
The lazy yawning drone. I this infer,
That many things having full reference⎫   205
To one consent may work contrariously,⎬

---

179 *advised* wise.   180-1 *though high . . . in one consent* though composed of various ranks and divided into different functions (like "parts" in a musical composition), acts in perfect harmony.   182 *Congreeing* agreeing mutually. *close* The word is used in the musical sense.   183 *True* Q¹; not in F¹ and probably an actor's interpolation.   186 *butt* target (in archery).   189 *The act of order* the method and operations of orderly, well-regulated society and government [K].   191 *correct* punish offenders.   193 *in* with.   194 *Make boot upon* plunder.   197 *majesty* royal office (Q¹; F¹: "Maiesties").   199 *civil* well-behaved, peaceable and orderly [K].   200 *mechanic* Almost always used in Elizabethan England of humble toilers, with a suggestion of contempt or pity or condescension [K].   202 *sad-ey'd* serious-eyed — not "sorrowful" [K].   203 *executors* executioners.   205-6 *having full . . .*

As many arrows <u>loosed several ways</u>
Come to one mark, as many <u>ways</u> meet in one town,
As many fresh streams meet in one salt sea,
As many lines close in the <u>dial's</u> centre;   210
So may a thousand actions, once <u>afoot</u>,
<u>End</u> in one purpose, and be all well <u>borne</u>
<u>Without defeat</u>. Therefore to France, my liege!
Divide your happy England into four,
Whereof take you one quarter into France,   215
And you <u>withal</u> shall make all Gallia shake.
If we, with thrice such <u>powers</u> left at home,
Cannot defend our own doors from the dog,
Let us be worried, and our nation lose
The name of hardiness and <u>policy</u>.   220

KING.   Call in the messengers sent from the Dauphin.

[*Exeunt some* Attendants.]

Now are we well <u>resolv'd</u>, and by God's help
And yours, the noble sinews of our power,
France being ours, we'll bend it to our awe,
Or break it all to pieces. <u>Or there</u> we'll sit,   225
Ruling in large and ample <u>empery</u>
O'er France and all her (almost) kingly dukedoms,
Or lay these bones in an <u>unworthy urn</u>,
<u>Tombless,</u> with no remembrance over them.
Either our history shall with full mouth   230
Speak freely of our acts, or else our grave,
<u>Like Turkish mute</u>, shall have a tongueless mouth,
<u>Not worshipp'd with a waxen epitaph.</u>

---

consent conducing altogether to one harmonious purpose [K].   207 *loosed several ways* shot from various directions.   208 *ways* roadways.   210 *dial's* sun-dial's.   211 *afoot* under way.   212 *End* Q¹; F¹: "And." *borne* carried out.   213 *Without defeat* without being thwarted in their individual operations [K].   216 *withal* with that.   217 *powers* forces, troops.   220 *policy* statesmanship.   222 *resolv'd* satisfied (as to our doubts and scruples).   224 *ours* rightfully mine.   *awe* obedience.   225 *Or there* either there.   226 *empery* sovereignty.   228 *unworthy urn* ignoble grave.   229 *Tombless* without a monument.   232 *Like Turkish mute* Certain Turkish slaves had their tongues cut out to insure the privacy of their masters.   233 *Not . . . epitaph* not even honoured (worshipp'd) with an epitaph in wax (let alone one in stone or brass).

Enter Ambassadors *of France,* [*attended*].

Now are we well prepar'd to know the pleasure
Of our fair cousin Dauphin; for we hear　　　　235
Your greeting is from him, not from the King.

AMBASSADOR. May't please your Majesty to give us leave
　　　　Freely to render what we have in charge;
　　　　Or shall we sparingly show you far off
　　　　The Dauphin's meaning, and our embassy?　　　240

KING.　　We are no tyrant, but a Christian king,
　　　　Unto whose grace our passion is as subject
　　　　As are our wretches fett'red in our prisons.
　　　　Therefore with frank and with uncurbed plainness
　　　　Tell us the Dauphin's mind.

AMBASSADOR.　　　　　　　　　Thus then, in few:　　245
　　　　Your Highness, lately sending into France,
　　　　Did claim some certain dukedoms, in the right
　　　　Of your great predecessor, King Edward the Third.
　　　　In answer of which claim, the Prince our master
　　　　Says that you savour too much of your youth,　　250
　　　　And bids you be advis'd. There's naught in France
　　　　That can be with a nimble galliard won;
　　　　You cannot revel into dukedoms there.
　　　　He therefore sends you, meeter for your spirit,
　　　　This tun of treasure; and, in lieu of this,　　255
　　　　Desires you let the dukedoms that you claim

238 *render . . . charge* report what we have been ordered to say.　239 *sparingly . . . off* indicate politely in general rather than specific terms.　242 *grace* virtue, Christian self-control [K].　243 *fett'red* The passions are thought of as here under control as much as prisoners are in their cells [K].　245 *in few* in few words, briefly.　251 *be advis'd* consider carefully.　252 *galliard* a lively dance. The Dauphin is reminding King Henry of his reputation as a reveller.　254 *meeter for your spirit* as being more appropriate to your disposition [K].　255 *tun* barrel. *in lieu of* in return for.　258 *Tennis balls* The implication is that King Henry is more fit for a tennis court than a battlefield.　259 *pleasant* inclined to practical joking.　261 *When we have match'd* In what follows the King uses rather elaborately the technical language of court tennis [K].　263 *strike . . . the hazard* (a) cause his father to risk his crown (b) hit his father's crown, like a tennis ball, into the hazard, a technical term for an opening in the wall surrounding the court; when the ball was hit into the hazard, a point was scored.　264 *wrangler* oppo-

	Hear no more of you. This the Dauphin speaks.	
KING.	What treasure, uncle?	
EXE.	Tennis balls, my liege.	
KING.	We are glad the Dauphin is so pleasant with us.	

His present and your pains we thank you for.   260
When we have match'd our rackets to these balls,
We will in France (by God's grace) play a set
Shall strike his father's crown into the hazard.
Tell him he hath made a match with such a wrangler
That all the courts of France will be disturb'd   265
With chases. And we understand him well,
How he comes o'er us with our wilder days,
Not measuring what use we made of them.
We never valu'd this poor seat of England,
And therefore, living hence, did give ourself   270
To barbarous license; as 'tis ever common
That men are merriest when they are from home.
But tell the Dauphin I will keep my state,
Be like a king, and show my sail of greatness,
When I do rouse me in my throne of France.   275
For that I have laid by my majesty
And plodded like a man for working days,
But I will rise there with so full a glory
That I will dazzle all the eyes of France,
Yea, strike the Dauphin blind to look on us.   280
And tell the pleasant Prince this mock of his
Hath turn'd his balls to gunstones, and his soul

---

nent.   266 *chases* (a) pursuits — of fleeing soldiers (b) lost points in tennis. A "chase" was literally a double bounce of the ball.   267 *comes o'er us with* reproaches us with, reminds us of with derision.   269 *seat* throne.   270 *living hence* i.e. living out of England. The King means that his thoughts were ever in France, "since our real residence was not in England — since, when we were in England, we were really away from home, France being our home" [K].   273 *keep my state* maintain my royal dignity [K].   274 *sail* swelling power.   275 *When I . . . France* "Rouse" suggests the alert attitude of one who, while sitting, is yet ready at any moment to spring to his feet [K].   276–7 *For that . . . working days* for that purpose, to conquer France, I temporarily laid aside my royalty and acted like an ordinary working man. Thus the King explains his youthful behaviour.   278 *rise there* The comparison of the king to the sun is conventional.   282 *gunstones* Cannon balls were originally made of stone, not metal [K].

Shall stand sore <u>charged</u> for the <u>wasteful</u> vengeance
That shall fly with them; for many a thousand widows
Shall this his mock mock out of their dear husbands,   285
Mock mothers from their sons, mock castles down;
And some are yet <u>ungotten</u> and unborn
That shall have cause to curse the Dauphin's scorn.
<u>But this lies all within the will of God</u>,
To whom I do appeal, and in whose name,   290
Tell you the Dauphin, I am coming on,
To venge me as I may and to put forth
My rightful hand in a well-hallow'd cause.
So get you hence in peace. And tell the Dauphin
His jest will savour but of shallow wit   295
When thousands weep more than did laugh at it.
<u>Convey</u> them with safe conduct. Fare you well.

                      Exeunt Ambassadors.

EXE.   This was a merry message.

KING.   We hope to make the sender blush at it.
Therefore, my lords, <u>omit no happy hour</u>   300
That may give furth'rance to our expedition;
For we have now no thought in us but France,
Save those to God, that run before our business.
Therefore let our <u>proportions</u> for these wars
Be soon collected, and all things thought upon   305
That may with reasonable swiftness add
More feathers to our wings; for, <u>God before</u>,
We'll chide this Dauphin at his father's door.
Therefore let every man now <u>task his thought</u>
<u>That</u> this fair action may on foot be brought.   *Exeunt.* 310

---

283 *charged* burdened with guilt or responsibility [K].   *wasteful* devastating.   287
ungotten not yet conceived.   289 *But this . . . God* The King has shown a certain
amount of excitement, but now he masters it and resumes his original solemnity
of demeanour. This appeal to God would of course be impossible but for the
elaborate exposition of the ecclesiastics in the preceding scene. They have made out
that this war is an assertion of a sacred right, that it is indeed a kind of holy war
[K].   297 *Convey* escort.   300 *omit . . . hour* lose no favourable opportunity.
303 *run before* precede. He means that all of his actions are preceded by prayers to
God.   304 *proportions* levies of men.   307 *God before* God going before, under
the guidance of God, with God's help. An old phrase, not to be confounded with
"before God" [K].   309 *task his thought* tax his mental powers.   310 *That* so that.

[Act Two]

◇◇

Flourish. Enter Chorus.

Now all the youth of England are on fire,
And silken dalliance in the wardrobe lies.
Now thrive the armourers, and honour's thought
Reigns solely in the breast of every man.
They sell the pasture now to buy the horse,   5
Following the mirror of all Christian kings
With winged heels, as English Mercuries.
For now sits Expectation in the air
And hides a sword, from hilts unto the point,
With crowns imperial, crowns, and coronets   10
Promis'd to Harry and his followers.
The French, advis'd by good intelligence
Of this most dreadful preparation,
Shake in their fear and with pale policy
Seek to divert the English purposes.   15

II. CHORUS. 2 *silken dalliance* social pleasure, which has been put off with the robes of silk appropriate to it [κ].   3 *honour's thought* thoughts of honour (to be won in battle).   6 *mirror of all Christian kings* ideal or model to be emulated by all Christian kings. The term "mirror" is often used in this sense.   7 *winged . . . Mercuries* Mercury, the messenger of the gods in Greek mythology, is always depicted with winged sandals and helmet.   9 *hilts* hilt. The plural is common because each of the parts of the hilt in our sense was called a hilt [κ].   10 *crowns imperial* such crowns as are worn by those who rule over more than one kingdom — such as Henry hopes to attain by his conquest of France. This is contrasted with the "crowns" worn by ordinary kings and the "coronets" worn by mere noblemen.   12 *intelligence* spies.   14 *pale policy* diplomacy or intrigue motivated by fear.

O England! <u>model to</u> thy inward greatness,
Like little body with a mighty heart,
What mightst thou do that honour <u>would thee do</u>,
Were all thy children <u>kind and natural</u>!
But see <u>thy fault</u>! France hath in thee found out   20
A nest of <u>hollow</u> <u>bosoms</u>, which he fills
With treacherous crowns; and three corrupted men —
One, <u>Richard Earl of Cambridge</u>, and the second,
Henry Lord Scroop of Masham, and the third,
Sir Thomas Grey, knight, of Northumberland —   25
Have, for the <u>gilt</u> of France (O guilt indeed!)
Confirm'd conspiracy with <u>fearful</u> France,
And by their hands <u>this grace of kings</u> must die,
If hell and treason hold their promises,
Ere he take ship for France, and in Southampton.   30
Linger your patience on, and well digest
Th' abuse of distance. <u>Force a play</u>!
The sum is paid, the traitors are agreed,
The King is set from London, and the scene
Is now transported, gentles, to Southampton.   35
There is the playhouse now, there must you sit,
And thence to France shall we convey you safe
And bring you back, charming the narrow seas
To give you gentle <u>pass</u>; for, if we may,
We'll not <u>offend one stomach</u> with our play.   40

16 *model to* miniature representation of. The physical country of England is conceived of as small when compared with the vast spirit of English greatness, and at
the same time as a small replica of that spirit. The following line makes this meaning clear.   18 *would thee do* would have thee do.   19 *kind and natural* The
words are virtually synonymous: "moved by natural feeling, obeying the laws of
nature, thus displaying true filial feeling."   20 *thy fault* Englishmen were regu-
larly accused of treachery in the Middle Ages because of their frequent revolts
against their kings [K].   21 *hollow* (a) treacherous (b) empty. *bosoms* (a) hearts
(b) garments where "crowns" in the sense of "gold coins" would be kept. To put
money in one's bosom is a common expression.   23 *Richard Earl of Cambridge*
younger son of Edmund Langley, Duke of York. By his marriage to Anne Mortimer,
he combined the claims to the throne of the second and fourth sons of King Edward
III. His own son, Richard Duke of York, was to press that claim during the reign
of Henry VI. The present act of treason thus foreshadows the Wars of the Roses
which are to come.   26 *gilt* The pun on "gilt" and "guilt" was so common in the
Elizabethan time that it may almost be called an idiom. Of course it was not intended to raise a laugh [K].   27 *fearful* frightened.   28 *this grace of kings* this

But, till the King come forth, and not till then,
Unto Southampton do we shift our scene.   *Exit.*

◇◇◇◇◇◇◇◇◇◇◇◇◇◇◇◇◇

[SCENE I. *London. A street.*]

Enter Corporal Nym *and* Lieutenant Bardolph.

BARD. Well met, Corporal Nym.

NYM. Good morrow, Lieutenant Bardolph.

BARD. What, are <u>Ancient</u> Pistol and you friends yet?

NYM. <u>For my part</u>, I care not. I say little; but when time shall
serve, there shall be smiles — but that shall be as it may.   5
I dare not fight; but I will <u>wink</u> and hold out mine
<u>iron</u>. It is a simple one; but <u>what though</u>? It will toast
cheese, and it will endure cold as another man's sword
will — and there's an end.

BARD. I will bestow a breakfast to make you friends, and we'll   10
be all three <u>sworn brothers</u> to France. Let't be so, good
Corporal Nym.

NYM. Faith, I will live so long as I may, that's the certain of
it; and when I cannot live any longer, I will do as I
may. That is <u>my rest</u>, that is the <u>rendezvous</u> of it.   15

BARD. It is certain, Corporal, that he is married to Nell

honour of kings, this person who confers honour on the kingly station [K].   31–2
digest . . . distance accept our violation of the unity of place.   32 *Force a play*
by the violent exercise of your imagination, fill out those acts in the play which
we cannot represent [K].   39 *pass* passage. The English Channel was proverbially
rough.   40 *offend one stomach* (a) offend one person's taste   (b) cause one person
to be seasick.

II.i. 3 *Ancient* ensign, standard-bearer.   4 *For my part* Nym's style of talking
is that of the person who says less than he means, indulging in awful threats of
what he means to do [K].   4–5 *when time . . . smiles* i.e. I will make up my
quarrel with Pistol when the proper time comes, but not before [K].   6 *wink* shut
my eyes. 7 *iron* sword.   7 *what though* what of it. All that follows is in the same
mood of awful hinting and ironical threatening [K].   11 *sworn brothers* brethren
in arms — after the old fashion of taking an oath to stand by each other and share
good fortune and bad alike [K]. There is a suggestion also of the "fraternity of
thieves."   15 *my rest* what I have determined. The expression is from the game of
"Primero." *rendezvous* end, total (literally, "the last resort").

　　　　Quickly, and certainly she did you wrong, for you were
　　　　troth-plight to her.

NYM.　I cannot tell. Things must be as they may. Men may
　　　　sleep, and they may have their throats about them at　20
　　　　that time, and some say knives have edges. It must be
　　　　as it may. Though patience be a tired mare, yet she will
　　　　plod. There must be conclusions. Well, I cannot tell.

　　　　　　　　　Enter Pistol *and* Hostess Quickly.

BARD.　Here comes Ancient Pistol and his wife. Good Corporal,
　　　　be patient here.　25

NYM.　How now, mine host Pistol?

PIST.　Base tyke, call'st thou me host?
　　　　Now by this hand I swear I scorn the term;
　　　　Nor shall my Nell keep lodgers!

HOST.　No, by my troth, not long; for we cannot lodge and　30
　　　　board a dozen or fourteen gentlewomen that live
　　　　honestly by the prick of their needles but it will be
　　　　thought we keep a bawdy house straight. [Nym *and*
　　　　Pistol *draw.*] O well-a-day, Lady, if he be not drawn
　　　　now! We shall see wilful adultery and murder com-　35
　　　　mitted.

BARD.　Good Lieutenant — good Corporal — offer nothing here.

NYM.　Pish!

PIST.　Pish for thee, Iceland dog! thou prick-ear'd cur of
　　　　Iceland!　40

---

18 *troth-plight* engaged to be married.　19 *I cannot tell* Nym still threatens with
an affectation of saying less than he means. In what follows he suggests that he
may cut Pistol's throat sometime if Pistol has it with him when he is asleep, as
men occasionally do [K].　22–3 *Though patience . . . plod* though I am almost at
the end of my patience, yet it will last a little longer. Still, there must be conclusions, i.e. the end must come sometime, and then let Pistol look out for himself
[K].　*mare* Q¹; F¹: "name."　26 *How . . . Pistol* Q¹; F¹, K add the line to Bardolph's
speech. That Q¹ must be correct is made clear by what follows.　27 *tyke* hound.
34 *drawn* with his sword out (HANMER; F¹: "hewne," which some editors retain as
meaning "cut down").　37 *offer nothing* offer no offence — don't fight.　39 *Iceland
dog* There was, and is, a kind of terrier called an Iceland terrier, with sharp ears.
We may imagine that Nym, in accordance with his secretive and darkly hinting
character, is represented as thin, with his hair cut short, and his ears thus appearing to stand out [K].　43 *shog off* move away.　44 *Solus* alone (theatre Latin).
Pistol takes the term as one of abuse.　45 *mervailous* marvellous — an old form,

HOST.   Good Corporal Nym, show thy valour, and put up your
        sword.

NYM.   Will you shog off? I would have you solus.

PIST.   "Solus," egregious dog? O viper vile!
        The "solus" in thy most mervailous face!   45
        The "solus" in thy teeth, and in thy throat,
        And in thy hateful lungs, yea, in thy maw, perdy!
        And, which is worse, within thy nasty mouth!
        I do retort the "solus" in thy bowels;
        For I can take, and Pistol's cock is up,   50
        And flashing fire will follow.

NYM.   I am not Barbason; you cannot conjure me. I have an
        humour to knock you indifferently well. If you grow
        foul with me, Pistol, I will scour you with my rapier,
        as I may, in fair terms. If you would walk off, I would   55
        prick your guts a little in good terms, as I may, and
        that's the humour of it.

PIST.   O braggard vile, and damned furious wight,
        The grave doth gape, and doting death is near.
        Therefore exhale!   60

BARD.   Hear me, hear me what I say! He that strikes the first
        stroke, I'll run him up to the hilts, as I am a soldier.

                                                        [Draws.]

PIST.   An oath of mickle might, and fury shall abate.

---

used by Pistol in accordance with his habit of quoting from plays and speaking in
the language of tragedy. The accent is on the second syllable [K].   47 *maw*
stomach. *perdy* by God (from the French "par dieu").   50 *take* (a) take offence;
understand, feel, and resent an insult [K] (b) take fire. *cock is up* is cocked, ready
for firing.   52 *Barbason* the name of a fiend. *conjure* lay, exorcise. Not being a
fiend, he is saying, he cannot be driven down with mere words.   53 *indifferently*
tolerably.   54 *scour* (a) thrash (b) cleanse — as a pistol was cleansed with a scouring
rod after it had been fired. The barrel of a fired pistol was said to be "foul".   55
fair terms good style.   57 *the humour of it* the way I feel about it.   58 *wight* man
(an archaic poetic term).   59 *doting death* The senseless epithet "doting" is used
by Pistol merely because of its alliterating with "death" [K]. But the notion of
Death as the grinning skeleton who loves his victims is very common.   60 *exhale*
breathe your last.   62 *hilts* sword hilt.   63 *mickle* great. Pistol is a coward, and
when Bardolph makes so vigorous a demonstration he is quite ready to shake
hands with Nym [K].

[Pistol *and* Nym *sheathe their swords.*]

Give me thy fist, thy forefoot to me give.
Thy spirits are most tall.   65

NYM.   I will cut thy throat one time or other in fair terms.
That is the humour of it.

PIST.   Couple a gorge!
That is the word. I thee defy again.
O hound of Crete, think'st thou my spouse to get?   70
No; to the spital go,
And from the powd'ring tub of infamy
Fetch forth the lazar kite of Cressid's kind,
Doll Tearsheet, she by name, and her espouse.
I have, and I will hold, the quondam Quickly   75
For the only she; and — pauca, there's enough.
Go to!

Enter the Boy.

BOY.   Mine host Pistol, you must come to my master — and
your hostess. He is very sick and would to bed. Good
Bardolph, put thy face between his sheets and do the   80
office of a warming pan. Faith, he's very ill.

BARD.   Away, you rogue!

HOST.   By my troth, he'll yield the crow a pudding one of these
days. The King has kill'd his heart. Good husband,
come home presently.   *Exit* [*with* Boy].   85

BARD.   Come, shall I make you two friends? We must to France
together. Why the devil should we keep knives to cut
one another's throats?

---

65 *tall* courageous.   68 *Couple a gorge,* Pistol's French for "couper la gorge," "to
cut the throat."   69 *thee defy* Q¹; F¹: "defie thee."   70 *O hound of Crete* Doubtless
a tag from some old play [K].   71 *spital* hospital.   72 *powd'ring tub* sweating tub
used for the treatment of venereal disease. Its name comes from the tub used to
"powder," i.e. "salt" beef for preservation.   73 *lazar kite* diseased whore.   *of
Cressid's kind* Cressida, the beloved of Troilus, became a symbol for the unfaithful
woman. In Robert Henryson's TESTAMENT OF CRESSEID she is depicted as a leper in
her old age, having been punished thus for her treachery to Troilus. This poem
was often printed in Shakespeare's day along with Chaucer's TROILUS AND CRISEYDE.
75 *quondam* former.   76 *For the only she* as the only woman in the world for me

PIST.	Let floods o'erswell, and fiends for food howl on!
NYM.	You'll pay me the eight shillings I won of you at betting? 90
PIST.	Base is the slave that pays.
NYM.	That now I will have. That's the humour of it.
PIST.	As manhood shall compound. Push home. *They draw.*
BARD.	By this sword, he that makes the first thrust, I'll kill him! By this sword, I will. [*Draws.*] 95
PIST.	"Sword" is an oath, and oaths must have their course.
	[*Sheathes his sword.*]
BARD.	Corporal Nym, an thou wilt be friends, be friends; an thou wilt not, why then be enemies with me too. Prithee put up.
NYM.	I shall have my eight shillings I won of you at betting? 100
PIST.	A noble shalt thou have, and present pay; And liquor likewise will I give to thee, And friendship shall combine, and brotherhood. I'll live by Nym, and Nym shall live by me. Is not this just? For I shall sutler be 105 Unto the camp, and profits will accrue. Give me thy hand. [*Nym sheathes his sword.*]
NYM.	I shall have my noble?
PIST.	In cash, most justly paid.
NYM.	Well then, that's the humour of't. [*They shake hands.*] 110

Enter Hostess.

[K]. *pauca* in few words.   76–7 *enough. Go to* POPE; F¹: "enough to go to."   79 *your* F¹; HANMER, K: "you."   80 *thy face* Bardolph has a flaming red face.   83 *yield . . . pudding* die on the gallows (a proverbial expression).   85 *presently* at once.   89 *Let floods . . . howl on* This sounds defiant. Pistol in his turn is now disinclined to accept reconciliation [K].   93 *As manhood shall compound* as courage shall determine.   96 *an oath* Pistol, once more cowed by Bardolph, pretends to give way in consideration of the sacredness of the oath which Bardolph has sworn [K].   97 *an* if.   100 *I shall . . . betting* Q¹; not in F¹.   101 *noble* one third of a pound.   *present pay* immediate payment (the rest presumably to follow later).   105 *sutler* seller of food and supplies.   110 *that's* F²; F¹: "that."

HOST.   As ever you came of women, come in quickly to Sir
         John. Ah, poor heart! he is so shak'd of a burning quo-
         tidian tertian that it is most lamentable to behold. Sweet
         men, come to him.

NYM.   The King hath run bad humours on the knight; that's   115
         the even of it.

PIST.   Nym, thou hast spoke the right.
         His heart is fracted and corroborate.

NYM.   The King is a good king, but it must be as it may. He
         passes some humours and careers.   120

PIST.   Let us condole the knight; for, lambkins, we will live.

                                                    Exeunt.

❖❖❖❖❖❖❖❖❖❖❖❖❖

            [SCENE II. *Southampton. A council chamber.*]

Enter Exeter, Bedford, *and* Westmoreland.

BED.   Fore God, his Grace is bold to trust these traitors.

EXE.   They shall be apprehended by-and-by.

WEST.   How smooth and even they do bear themselves,
         As if allegiance in their bosoms sat,
         Crowned with faith and constant loyalty!   5

BED.   The King hath note of all that they intend,
         By interception which they dream not of.

EXE.   Nay, but the man that was his bedfellow,

---

111 *came of* Q¹; F¹: "come of." 112–13 *quotidian tertian* In a quotidian ague the
fit came every day; in a tertian ague, every other day. The hostess has mixed her
terms, as usual [K]. 115 *hath run . . . the knight* has forced the knight to put
up with disagreeable treatment. "Humour," it will be seen, is Nym's pet word,
which he uses in all sorts of vague ways [K]. 118 *fracted* broken. *corroborate*
properly "strengthen," but misused by Pistol to mean "broken to pieces" [K]. 120
passes . . . careers makes people put up with various whims and queer courses of
action (more of Nym's peculiar dialect) [K]. 121 *condole* sympathize with. *for,
lambkins, we will live* This seems to have no logical connection with what precedes,
and probably is not intended to have any such connection [K].
   II.II. 5 *Crowned* The figure is that of allegiance as ruling their natures [K].   6

Whom he hath <u>dull'd and cloy'd</u> with gracious favours —
That he should, <u>for a foreign purse,</u> so sell   10
His sovereign's life to death and treachery!

> *Sound   trumpets.   Enter   the* King,
> Scroop, Cambridge, *and* Grey, [Lords,
> *and* Attendants].

KING.   Now sits the wind fair, and we will aboard.
          My Lord of Cambridge, and my kind Lord of Masham,
          And you, my gentle knight, <u>give me your thoughts</u>.
          Think you not that the <u>pow'rs</u> we bear with us   15
          Will cut their passage through the force of France,
          Doing the execution and the act
          For which we have <u>in head</u> assembled them?

SCROOP.   No doubt, my liege, if each man do his best.

KING.   I doubt not that, since we are well persuaded   20
          We carry not a heart with us from hence
          That <u>grows not in a fair consent</u> with ours,
          Nor leave not one behind that doth not wish
          Success and conquest to attend on us.

CAM.   Never was monarch better fear'd and lov'd   25
          Than is your Majesty. There's not, I think, a subject
          That sits in heart-grief and uneasiness
          Under the sweet shade of your government.

GREY.   True. Those that were your father's enemies
          Have <u>steep'd their galls in honey</u> and do serve you   30
          With hearts <u>create of</u> duty and of zeal.

KING.   We therefore have great cause of thankfulness,

note knowledge.   8 *bedfellow* bosom friend.   9 *dull'd and cloy'd* satisfied and
surfeited. The two words are virtually synonymous.   10 *for a foreign purse*
Holinshed and Hall both record that the conspirators hoped to place Edmund
Mortimer, Earl of March, upon the throne. They are thus not entirely motivated
by foreign gold, although the chroniclers report this as a motive as well.   14 *give
me your thoughts* let me know what you think.   15 *pow'rs* troops.   18 *in head*
as an armed force.   22 *grows . . . consent* does not act in perfect harmony with
our sentiments [K].   30 *steep'd . . . honey* changed their resentment to affection.
"Gall" is frequently used for resentment or the capacity for resentment [K].   31
create of composed of.

> And shall forget the office of our hand
> Sooner than quittance of desert and merit
> According to the weight and worthiness.   35

SCROOP. So service shall with steeled sinews toil,
> And labour shall refresh itself with hope,
> To do your Grace incessant services.

KING. We judge no less. Uncle of Exeter,
> Enlarge the man committed yesterday   40
> That rail'd against our person. We consider
> It was excess of wine that set him on,
> And on his more advice, we pardon him.

SCROOP. That's mercy, but too much security.
> Let him be punish'd, sovereign, lest example   45
> Breed (by his sufferance) more of such a kind.

KING. O, let us yet be merciful!

CAM. So may your Highness, and yet punish too.

GREY. Sir,
> You show great mercy if you give him life   50
> After the taste of much correction.

KING. Alas, your too much love and care of me
> Are heavy orisons 'gainst this poor wretch!
> If little faults proceeding on distemper
> Shall not be wink'd at, how shall we stretch our eye   55
> When capital crimes, chew'd, swallow'd, and digested,
> Appear before us? We'll yet enlarge that man,
> Though Cambridge, Scroop, and Grey, in their dear care
> And tender preservation of our person,

---

33 *shall . . . hand* shall forget how to use our hands. The phrase is suggested by
the biblical "If I forget thee, O Jerusalem, let my right hand forget her cunning"
(PSALMS, CXXXVII, 5) [K].   34 *quittance* payment, reward.   40 *Enlarge* set free.
43 *on his more advice* now that he has had more time to consider his actions.
44 *security* carelessness, overconfidence.   46 *his sufferance* the toleration of his
act.   51 *correction* punishment.   53 *heavy orisons* weighty prayers.   54 *proceed-
ing on distemper* resulting from physical disorder — here the physical disturbance
caused by drunkenness. A man is in temper when all the four humours are
properly balanced in his constitution. Any undue disturbance of this balance re-
sults in distemper, disorder of mind or body [K].   55 *wink'd at* disregarded.
To "wink" is to "close the eyes." *stretch our eye* contemplate with eyes wide

Would have him punish'd. And now to our French
    causes.   60
Who are the late commissioners?

CAM.   I one, my lord.
Your Highness bade me ask for it to-day.

SCROOP.   So did you me, my liege.

GREY.   And I, my royal sovereign.   65

KING.   Then, Richard Earl of Cambridge, there is yours;
There yours, Lord Scroop of Masham; and, Sir Knight,
Grey of Northumberland, this same is yours.
Read them, and know I know your worthiness.
My Lord of Westmoreland, and uncle Exeter,   70
We will aboard to-night. — Why how now, gentlemen?
What see you in those papers that you lose
So much complexion? — Look ye, how they change!
Their cheeks are paper. — Why, what read you there
That hath so cowarded and chas'd your blood   75
Out of appearance?

CAM.   I do confess my fault,
And do submit me to your Highness' mercy.

GREY, SCROOP.   To which we all appeal.

KING.   The mercy that was quick in us but late,
By your own counsel is suppress'd and kill'd.   80
You must not dare (for shame) to talk of mercy;
For your own reasons turn into your bosoms
As dogs upon their masters, worrying you.
See you, my princes and my noble peers,
These English monsters! My Lord of Cambridge here —   85

---

open.   57 *yet* in spite of all you say [K].   61 *the late commissioners* the persons
lately appointed to act as a commission in England in place of the King while
he is absent in France [K].   63 *for it* for a place on the commission.   66 *yours* i.e.
your commission. The King hands to each of the traitors an order of arrest on the
charge of high treason [K].   72–3 *lose . . . complexion* turn pale.   74 *paper* (a)
pale as paper (b) like paper in that they may be read.   75 *hath* Q¹; F¹: "haue."
76 *appearance* sight.   *fault* crime.   79 *quick* alive.   82 *your own reasons* i.e.
the reasons that they have given for the punishment of the drunken railer [K].
85 *monsters* monstrosities, freaks — such as were often displayed in Elizabethan
side shows.

You know how apt our love was to accord
To furnish him with all appertinents
Belonging to his honour; and this man
Hath, for a few light crowns, lightly conspir'd
And sworn unto the practices of France   90
To kill us here in Hampton; to the which
This knight, no less for bounty bound to us
Than Cambridge is, hath likewise sworn. But O,
What shall I say to thee, Lord Scroop, thou cruel,
Ingrateful, savage, and inhuman creature?   95
Thou that didst bear the key of all my counsels,
That knew'st the very bottom of my soul,
That (almost) mightst have coin'd me into gold,⎱
Wouldst thou have practis'd on me for thy use ⎰
May it be possible that foreign hire   100
Could out of thee extract one spark of evil
That might annoy my finger? 'Tis so strange
That, though the truth of it stands off as gross
As black and white, my eye will scarcely see it.
Treason and murder ever kept together,   105
As two yoke-devils sworn to either's purpose,
Working so grossly in a natural cause
That admiration did not whoop at them;
But thou ('gainst all proportion) didst bring in
Wonder to wait on treason and on murder;   110
And whatsoever cunning fiend it was

---

86 *apt* ready. Much more active in sense than in modern English [ĸ]. *accord* consent.   87 *him* F²; not in F¹. *appertinents* appurtenances.   89 *lightly* with levity, easily, without consideration or scruple. The pun expresses contempt [ĸ].   90 *practices* plots.   96 *counsels* secrets.   98-9 *That (almost) . . . thy use* The King plays on the fact that Scroop had served as Lord Treasurer. "Use" carries the meaning of "interest" in the monetary sense, as well as of "advantage."   102 *my finger* even my finger.   103 *stands off as gross* appears as obvious.   105 *ever kept* have always worked.   106 *two . . . purpose* two fellow workers each entirely dedicated to the same purpose. A "yoke-fellow" is a fellow worker.   107 *Working . . . cause* operating together with such obvious fitness in carrying out the purposes to which they were both inclined by nature [ĸ].   108 *admiration . . . them* wonder never cried out at them. The general thought is that nobody has ever been surprised at seeing murder and treason on the part of the same person, since they are natural associates, but that now at least it is astonishing that this particular traitor, Lord Scroop, should also be a murderer [ĸ].   109 *'gainst all proportion* contrary to all the fitness of things [ĸ].   110 *wait on* accompany.   112 *preposterously* monstrously, against nature [ĸ].   113 *Hath got the voice* has won the vote, is generally acknowledged.   114 *All* HANMER; F¹: "And." *suggest* tempt.   115 *botch . . . damnation* patch up a crime which deserves damnation with all

That wrought upon thee so preposterously
Hath got the voice in hell for excellence.
All other devils that suggest by treasons
Do botch and bungle up damnation   115
With patches, colours, and with forms being fetch'd
From glist'ring semblances of piety;
But he that temper'd thee bade thee stand up,
Gave thee no instance why thou shouldst do treason,
Unless to dub thee with the name of traitor.   120
If that same demon that hath gull'd thee thus
Should with his lion gait walk the whole world,
He might return to vasty Tartar back
And tell the legions, "I can never win
A soul so easy as that Englishman's."   125
O, how hast thou with jealousy infected
The sweetness of affiance! Show men dutiful?
Why, so didst thou. Seem they grave and learned?
Why, so didst thou. Come they of noble family?
Why, so didst thou. Seem they religious?   130
Why, so didst thou. Or are they spare in diet,
Free from gross passion or of mirth or anger,
Constant in spirit, not swerving with the blood,
Garnish'd and deck'd in modest complement,
Not working with the eye without the ear,   135
And but in purged judgment trusting neither?
Such and so finely bolted didst thou seem;

---

sorts of pretenses to make it look virtuous [K].   116 *colours* pretexts.   *forms*
mere outward appearances.   116–17 *being fetch'd . . . piety* made to resemble
the bright appearance of piety. Beneath the passage runs the clothes metaphor.
A "botcher" is a mender of old clothes, and "patches," "colours," and "forms" are
materials with which a tailor works.   118 *temper'd thee* worked thee to his will;
induced thee to commit this crime [K].   *bade thee stand up* abruptly ordered
thee to support his cause.   119 *instance* reason.   121 *gull'd* misled.   122 *with his
lion . . . world* A biblical figure. Cf. I PETER, V, 8: "Your adversary the devil, as a
roaring lion, walketh about, seeking whom he may devour" [K].   123 *Tartar* the
pit of Tartarus, i.e. hell.   124 *legions* companies of devils.   126 *jealousy* suspicion.
127 *affiance* trust.   *Show* appear.   128 *grave* dignified.   132 *or of* either of.   133
with the blood at the dictates of passion.   134 *Garnish'd . . . complement* furnished with every appearance of moderation and self-control. "Complement" often
means "outward appearance" [K].   135 *Not working . . . ear* not acting rashly
on the basis of what you see without some evidence that has come by ear [K].
136 *but in . . . neither* trusting neither the evidence of the eye nor that of the ear
except on the basis of well-tried and clarified consideration [K].   137 *so finely
bolted* of so fine (literally, so thoroughly sifted) a nature [K].

And thus thy fall hath left a kind of blot
To mark the full-fraught man and best indu'd
With some suspicion. I will weep for thee;   140
For this revolt of thine, methinks, is like
Another fall of man. Their faults are open.
Arrest them to the answer of the law;
And God acquit them of their practices!

EXE.   I arrest thee of high treason by the name of Richard 145
Earl of Cambridge.
I arrest thee of high treason by the name of Henry Lord
Scroop of Masham.
I arrest thee of high treason by the name of Thomas
Grey, knight, of Northumberland.   150

SCROOP.   Our purposes God justly hath discover'd,
And I repent my fault more than my death,
Which I beseech your Highness to forgive,
Although my body pay the price of it.

CAM.   For me, the gold of France did not seduce,⎫   155
Although I did admit it as a motive   ⎬
The sooner to effect what I intended.   ⎭
But God be thanked for prevention,
Which I in sufferance heartily will rejoice,
Beseeching God, and you, to pardon me.   160

GREY.   Never did faithful subject more rejoice
At the discovery of most dangerous treason
Than I do at this hour joy o'er myself,
Prevented from a damned enterprise.
My fault, but not my body, pardon, sovereign.   165

KING.   God quit you in his mercy! Hear your sentence.
You have conspir'd against our royal person,

---

139 *mark the* THEOBALD; F¹: "mark thee." *full-fraught* fully laden. *indu'd* endowed.
142 *open* fully disclosed.   144 *acquit . . . practices* forgive them for their plots.
147 *Henry* Q¹; F¹: "Thomas."   151 *discover'd* revealed.   155–7 *For me . . . I intended* The true motive of the conspiracy, as Hall and Holinshed make clear,
was to place upon the throne Edmund Mortimer, Earl of March who, as the
descendant of Lionel of Clarence had a better claim to the throne than King Henry.
Since Edmund Mortimer had no children, the succession would then pass to the
children of Richard Earl of Cambridge who was married to his sister, Anne
Mortimer.   158 *prevention* my having been forestalled.   159 *Which I in* F²;

Join'd with an enemy proclaim'd, and from his coffers
Receiv'd the golden earnest of our death;
Wherein you would have sold your king to slaughter,   170
His princes and his peers to servitude,
His subjects to oppression and contempt,
And his whole kingdom into desolation.
Touching our person, seek we no revenge,
But we our kingdom's safety must so tender,   175
Whose ruin you have sought, that to her laws
We do deliver you. Get you therefore hence
(Poor miserable wretches) to your death;
The taste whereof God of his mercy give
You patience to endure, and true repentance   180
Of all your dear offences! Bear them hence.

> *Exeunt* [Cambridge, Scroop, *and* Grey,
> *guarded*].

Now, lords, for France; the enterprise whereof
Shall be to you as us, like glorious.
We doubt not of a fair and lucky war,
Since God so graciously hath brought to light   185
This dangerous treason, lurking in our way
To hinder our beginnings. We doubt not now
But every rub is smoothed on our way.
Then, forth, dear countrymen. Let us deliver
Our puissance into the hand of God,   190
Putting it straight in expedition.
Cheerly to sea; the signs of war advance.
No king of England, if not King of France!

> *Flourish. Exeunt.*

F¹: "Which in." *sufferance* my suffering.   166 *quit* acquit, absolve.   169 *golden earnest* partial payment of gold made in advance to bind the bargain.   174 *Touching* with regard to.   175 *tender* hold, regard.   176 *you have sought* Q¹; F¹: "you sought."   181 *dear offences* heinous offences. "Dear" is used of anything that affects one nearly, whether of love or hate, joy or sorrow [K].   183 *like* equally.   188 *rub* impediment (a term from the game of bowls).   190 *puissance* troops (trisyllabic).   191 *straight in expedition* immediately into motion (with a sense of "haste").   192 *signs* ensigns, banners. *advance* raise up.   193 *No king . . . of France* This is the watchword of the King's foreign expedition [K].

◇◇◇◇◇◇◇◇◇◇◇◇◇◇◇◇

[SCENE III.
London. Before the Boar's Head Tavern, Eastcheap.]

Enter Pistol, Nym, Bardolph, Boy, *and* Hostess.

HOST.   Prithee, honey-sweet husband, let me bring thee to
        Staines.

PIST.   No; for my manly heart doth ern.
        Bardolph, be blithe; Nym, rouse thy vaunting veins;
        Boy, bristle thy courage up; for Falstaff he is dead,   5
        And we must ern therefore.

BARD.   Would I were with him, wheresome'er he is, either in
        heaven or in hell!

HOST.   Nay sure, he's not in hell! He's in Arthur's bosom, if
        ever man went to Arthur's bosom. 'A made a finer end,   10
        and went away an it had been any christom child. 'A
        parted ev'n just between twelve and one, ev'n at the
        turning o' th' tide. For after I saw him fumble with
        the sheets, and play with flowers, and smile upon his
        fingers' ends, I knew there was but one way; for his   15
        nose was as sharp as a pen, and 'a babbled of green
        fields. "How now, Sir John?" quoth I. "What, man? be
        o' good cheer." So 'a cried out "God, God, God!" three
        or four times. Now I, to comfort him, bid him 'a should

---

II.III. An extraordinary scene — beyond question one of the most wonderful in Shakespeare. In mourning for Falstaff all these comic characters speak in accordance with their several whimsicalities of style and manner — Pistol rants, alliterates and defies logic, the Hostess mixes up her words and speaks with ludicrous ambiguity, the Page pokes fun at Bardolph's nose and Bardolph resents it with his usual irascibility. Nothing could be more wildly comic than what is said; yet the general effect is that of almost unendurable pathos [K].   1 *bring* accompany.   2 *Staines* a town on the Thames, on the way to Southampton.   3 *ern* grieve.   4 *vaunting veins* high spirits.   10 *Arthur's bosom* The Hostess confuses Abraham's bosom (LUKE, XVI, 22) with the myth of King Arthur in the earthly paradise of Avalon [K].   *a finer end* i.e. than going to hell.   11 *christom child* newly christened child. During the first month after baptism infants wore a chrism-cloth.   12-13 *the turning o' th' tide* i.e. the moment when the time changes from night to day. "Tide" often means "time" (which is, indeed, its original sense). Many think that "tide" is here used of the sea, and it is true that there is a belief that people die at ebb tide rather than at flood [K].   14 *play with flowers* pick at the bed-

    not think of God; I hop'd there was no need to trouble 20
    himself with any such thoughts yet. So 'a bade me lay
    more clothes on his feet. I put my hand into the bed
    and felt them, and they were as cold as any stone. Then
    I felt to his knees, and <u>so upward</u> and upward, and all
    was as cold as any stone. 25

NYM.   They say he cried out <u>of sack</u>.

HOST.   Ay, that 'a did.

BARD.   And of women.

HOST.   Nay, that 'a did not.

BOY.   Yes, that 'a did, and said they were devils <u>incarnate.</u> *(a)* 30

HOST.   'A could never abide carnation; 'twas a colour he never
    lik'd.

BOY.   'A said once the devil would have him about women.

HOST.   'A did in some sort, indeed, <u>handle</u> women; but then he
    was <u>rheumatic,</u> and talk'd of the Whore of Babylon. 35

BOY.   Do you not remember 'a saw a flea stick upon Bardolph's
    nose, and 'a said it was a black soul burning in <u>hellfire?</u>

BARD.   Well, <u>the fuel</u> is gone that maintain'd that fire. That's
    all the riches I got in his service.

NYM.   Shall we <u>shog</u>? The King will be gone from Southampton. 40

PIST.   Come, let's away. My love, give me thy lips.
    Look to my chattels and my <u>moveables.</u>

---

clothes, as if he were plucking flowers [K]. 14–15 *smile . . . ends* Falstaff held up his fingers and smiled at them, imagining that he was looking at the flowers he had plucked [K]. *ends* Q¹; F¹: "end." 16 *'a babbled* It was because Falstaff talked of green fields in his delirium that the Hostess knew that he was "playing with flowers." Otherwise she would not have given this interpretation to his picking at the coverlet [K] (THEOBALD; F¹: "A Table"). Few today would question this most brilliant and time-honoured of Shakespearean emendations. 24 *so upward* Q¹; F¹: "so vp-peer'd." 26 *of* against. *sack* sweet Spanish wine, Falstaff's favourite drink. 30 *incarnate* (a) in the flesh (b) in red, a colour traditionally worn by Elizabethan whores. 34 *handle* discuss. 35 *rheumatic* She probably means "lunatic," although the word was probably pronounced "romatic," thus preparing for the "Whore of Babylon," a popular expression used for the Roman Catholic Church. 37 *hellfire* Q¹; F¹: "Hell." 38 *the fuel* i.e. the liquor with which Falstaff had supplied Bardolph, thus contributing to the "fire" (redness) in his face. 40 *shog* move along. 42 *moveables* furniture.

Let senses rule. The word is "Pitch and pay."
Trust none;
For oaths are straws, men's faiths are wafer-cakes,   45
And Hold-fast is the only dog, my duck.
Therefore Caveto be thy counsellor.
Go, clear thy crystals. Yoke-fellows in arms,
Let us to France, like horse-leeches, my boys,
To suck, to suck, the very blood to suck!   50

BOY.   And that's but unwholesome food, they say.

PIST.   Touch her soft mouth, and march.

BARD.   Farewell, hostess.   [*Kisses her.*]

NYM.   I cannot kiss, that is the humour of it; but adieu!

PIST.   Let housewifery appear. Keep close, I thee command. 55

HOST.   Farewell! adieu!   *Exeunt.*

❖❖❖❖❖❖❖❖❖❖❖❖❖❖

[SCENE IV. *France. The* French King's *Palace.*]

Flourish. Enter the French King, *the* Dauphin, *the*
Dukes of Berri *and* Britain, [*the* Constable, *and
others*].

KING.   Thus comes the English with full power upon us,
And more than carefully it us concerns
To answer royally in our defences.
Therefore the Dukes of Berri and of Britain,
Of Brabant and of Orleans, shall make forth,   5

---

43 *Let senses rule* let prudence govern (in the management of the tavern) [K].
word Q¹; F¹: "world." *Pitch* plank down your money [K]. "Pitch and pay" was an
old expression for "No credit."   45 *wafer-cakes* i.e. easily broken.   46 *Hold-fast*
cf. the proverb, "Brag is a good dog, but Hold-fast is better" [K].   47 *Caveto*
beware, caution.   48 *clear thy crystals* wipe your eyes.   49 *like horse-leeches* cf.
PROVERBS, XXX,15: "The horse-leech hath two daughters, crying 'Give! give!'" [K].
51 *unwholesome food* The blood of animals was believed to be bad for the diges-
tion.   54 *I cannot kiss* The saturnine Nym has made up his quarrel with Pistol,
but he cannot bring himself to kiss his lost love [K].   55 *housewifery* prudent
management.   *Keep close* live retired, don't go about. These prudent counsels
from mine host Pistol are indescribably comic [K̇].

And you, Prince Dauphin, with all swift dispatch,
To line and new repair our towns of war
With men of courage and with means defendant;
For England his approaches makes as fierce
As waters to the sucking of a gulf.   10
It fits us then to be as provident
As fear may teach us out of late examples
Left by the fatal and neglected English
Upon our fields.

DAU.   My most redoubted father,
It is most meet we arm us 'gainst the foe;   15
For peace itself should not so dull a kingdom
(Though war nor no known quarrel were in question)
But that defences, musters, preparations
Should be maintain'd, assembled, and collected,
As were a war in expectation.   20
Therefore I say 'tis meet we all go forth
To view the sick and feeble parts of France;
And let us do it with no show of fear —
No, with no more than if we heard that England
Were busied with a Whitsun morris dance;   25
For, my good liege, she is so idly king'd,
Her sceptre so fantastically borne,
By a vain, giddy, shallow, humorous youth,
That fear attends her not.

CON.   O peace, Prince Dauphin!
You are too much mistaken in this king.   30
Question your Grace the late ambassadors,

II.IV. 4 *and of* F¹; κ: "and." 7 *line* strengthen, fortify. 8 *means defendant*
defensive measures. 10 *gulf* whirlpool. 12 *late examples* i.e. the battles of Crécy
(1346) and Poitiers (1356). 13 *fatal and neglected* fatally underrated (hendiadys).
14 *redoubted* feared, respected. 15 *meet we* fitting that we. 25 *Whitsun morris
dance* Whitsuntide was the time of spring festivities, among which the morris
dance was conspicuous [κ]. It was a grotesque dance in which the performers wore
bells and blackened their faces; since they were thought popularly to represent
Moors, the name "Moorish" or "morris" dance came into being. 26 *so idly
king'd* furnished with so vain and empty-headed a king [κ]. 27 *so fantastically
borne* borne by so fantastic a creature, by such a fop or buffoon [κ]. 28 *humorous*
capricious. 29 *attends* accompanies.

With what great state he heard their embassy,
How well supplied with noble counsellors,
How modest in exception, and withal
How terrible in constant resolution,   35
And you shall find his vanities forespent
Were but the outside of the Roman Brutus,
Covering discretion with a coat of folly;
As gardeners do with ordure hide those roots
That shall first spring and be most delicate.   40

DAU.   Well, 'tis not so, my Lord High Constable!
But though we think it so, it is no matter.
In cases of defence 'tis best to weigh
The enemy more mighty than he seems.
So the proportions of defence are fill'd;   45
Which of a weak and niggardly projection
Doth, like a miser, spoil his coat with scanting
A little cloth.

KING.   Think we King Harry strong;
And, princes, look you strongly arm to meet him.
The kindred of him hath been flesh'd upon us;   50
And he is bred out of that bloody strain
That haunted us in our familiar paths.
Witness our too much memorable shame
When Cressy battle fatally was struck,
And all our princes captiv'd, by the hand   55
Of that black name, Edward, Black Prince of Wales;
Whiles that his mountain sire — on mountain standing,
Up in the air, crown'd with the golden sun —
Saw his heroical seed, and smil'd to see him,

---

32 *great state* magnificent royal ceremony and bearing.   34 *modest in exception*
moderate, self-controlled, in taking exception, or objecting [K].   *withal* at the same
time.   35 *constant* firm.   36 *vanities forespent* past follies.   37-8 *Roman Brutus
. . . folly* Lucius Junius Brutus, the Liberator, appointed Consul in 509 B.C.,
pretended to be an idiot in order to protect himself from his uncle, King Tar-
quinius Superbus. He later helped expel the Tarquins from Rome.   *discretion*
wisdom.   39 *ordure* manure.   41 *Constable* the chief military officer of France
[K].   46 *of a weak . . . projection* if they are planned on a feeble and niggardly
scale [K].   47 *scanting* sparing.   50 *been flesh'd* drawn blood and become excited
by the taste of it. The figure is from hunting; dogs and hawks were trained to hunt
by the taste of flesh.   51 *strain* race, family.   52 *haunted* pursued.   57 *mountain*

Mangle the work of nature, and deface   60
The patterns that by God and by French fathers
Had twenty years been made. This is a stem
Of that victorious stock; and let us fear
The native mightiness and fate of him.

Enter a Messenger.

MESS.   Ambassadors from Harry King of England   65
Do crave admittance to your Majesty.

KING.   We'll give them present audience. Go, and bring them.

[*Exeunt* Messenger *and certain* Lords.]

You see this chase is hotly followed, friends.

DAU.   Turn head, and stop pursuit; for coward dogs
Most spend their mouths when what they seem to threaten 70
Runs far before them. Good my sovereign,
Take up the English short, and let them know
Of what a monarchy you are the head.
Self-love, my liege, is not so vile a sin
As self-neglecting.

Enter [Lords, *with*] Exeter [*and*
Train].

KING.   From our brother of England?   75

EXE.   From him, and thus he greets your Majesty:
He wills you, in the name of God Almighty,
That you devest yourself, and lay apart
The borrowed glories that by gift of heaven,
By law of nature and of nations, 'longs   80
To him and to his heirs — namely, the crown
And all wide-stretched honours that pertain

---

sire Edward III, born among the mountains of Wales [K]. 64 *The native . . .
fate of him* the great destiny which he has inherited.   67 *present* immediate.
69 *Turn head* stand at bay. A hunting term.   70 *Most spend their mouths* bark
loudest.   75 *of* F¹; not in Q¹, K.   80 *law of nature* The medieval concept of Natural Law held that there was a law operating in the universe which could be
perceived by men through the use of human reason; this law was a reflection of
divine law, to which it was subordinate and which could only be known by revelation. The law "of nations" was that enacted by men for their own government, and
it had to conform with Natural Law. Henry is asserting his claim by virtue of
every law, human and divine, believed to govern human affairs. *'longs* belongs.

By custom, and the ordinance of times,
Unto the crown of France. That you may know
'Tis no sinister nor no awkward claim,   85
Pick'd from the wormholes of long-vanish'd days,
Nor from the dust of old oblivion rak'd,
He sends you this most memorable line,

[*Gives a paper.*]

In every branch truly demonstrative;
Willing you overlook this pedigree;   90
And when you find him evenly deriv'd
From his most fam'd of famous ancestors,
Edward the Third, he bids you then resign
Your crown and kingdom, indirectly held
From him, the native and true challenger.   95

KING. Or else what follows?

EXE. Bloody constraint; for if you hide the crown
Even in your hearts, there will he rake for it.
Therefore in fierce tempest is he coming,
In thunder and in earthquake, like a Jove;   100
That, if requiring fail, he will compel;
And bids you, in the bowels of the Lord,
Deliver up the crown, and to take mercy
On the poor souls for whom this hungry war
Opens his vasty jaws; and on your head   105
Turning the widows' tears, the orphans' cries,
The dead men's blood, the pining maidens' groans,
For husbands, fathers, and betrothed lovers
That shall be swallowed in this controversy.
This is his claim, his threat'ning, and my message;   110

---

83 *the ordinance of times* ancient laws — especially the Salic Law [K].   85 *sinister* literally, "left-handed," and so "irregular," with special allusion to the "bar sinister," which is used in heraldry to denote illegitimate birth [K].   *awkward* literally, "back-handed," and so "indirect," "unlawful" [K].   86 *Pick'd* selected carefully (with a special conclusion in mind).   88 *line* pedigree.   89 *demonstrative* proving his claim.   90 *overlook* look over, examine.   91 *evenly* in lawful and regular succession — opposed to "sinister" and "awkward" in line 85 [K].   94 *indirectly* unjustly.   95 *challenger* claimant.   97 *constraint* compulsion, war.   99 *fierce* F¹, Q¹; DYCE, K: "fiery."   101 *That* so that.   *requiring* mere request.   102 *in the bowels of the Lord* by the compassion of the Lord. "In" is used in ad-

Unless the Dauphin be in presence here,
To whom expressly I bring greeting too.

KING.   <u>For us</u>, we will consider of this further.
To-morrow shall you bear our full intent
Back to our brother <u>of</u> England.

DAU.   <u>For</u> the Dauphin,   115
I stand here for him. What to him from England?

EXE.   Scorn and defiance, slight regard, contempt,
And anything that may not misbecome
The mighty sender, doth he prize you at.
Thus says my king: An if your father's Highness   120
Do not, in grant of all demands <u>at large</u>,
Sweeten the bitter mock you sent his Majesty,
He'll call you to so hot an answer of it
That caves and <u>womby vaultages</u> of France
Shall chide your trespass, and return your mock   125
In <u>second accent</u> of his <u>ordinance</u>.

DAU.   Say, if my father render fair return,
It is against my will; for I desire
Nothing but <u>odds</u> with England. To that end,
As matching to his youth and vanity,   130
I did present him with the <u>Paris balls.</u>

EXE.   He'll make your Paris <u>Louvre</u> shake for it,
Were it the mistress court of mighty Europe;
And be assur'd you'll find a difference,
As we his subjects have in wonder found,   135
Between <u>the promise of his greener days</u>
And these he <u>masters</u> now. Now he weighs time
Even to the utmost grain. That you shall read

---

jurations in the sense of "by." "Bowels" is a biblical word for "mercy," "compassion" [K].   105 *vasty* vast.   106 *Turning* F¹; Q¹, K: "Turns he."   107 *pining* Q¹; F¹: "priuy."   113 *For us* for my part.   115 *of* F¹; not in Q¹, K.   *For* as for. 121 *at large* in full.   124 *womby vaultages* hollow caverns.   126 *second accent* echo.   *ordinance* ordnance.   129 *odds* quarrel, controversy.   131 *Paris balls* tennis balls (an old name for them).   132 *Louvre* POPE; Q¹, F¹: "louer," indicating the Elizabethan pronunciation ("lover"), and giving point to the "mistress court" of the following line.   136 *the promise of his greener days* what his youth seemed to promise for the future.   137 *masters* possesses, controls.

In your own losses, if he stay in France.

KING.   To-morrow shall you know our mind at full.   140

EXE.   Dispatch us with all speed, lest that our king
Come here himself to question our delay;
For he is <u>footed</u> in this land already.

KING.   You shall be soon dispatch'd with fair conditions.
A night is but <u>small breath</u> and little pause   145
To answer matters of this consequence.

Flourish. Exeunt.

---

143 *footed* landed. Henry actually did not land in France until August 14, 1415, although Exeter's embassy took place in February.   145 *small breath* small breathing space, short time for consideration [ᴋ].

[Act Three]

◇◇◇

Enter Chorus.

Thus with imagin'd wing our swift scene flies,
In motion of no less celerity
Than that of thought. Suppose that you have seen
The well-appointed King at Hampton pier
Embark his royalty; and his brave fleet 5
With silken streamers the young Phœbus fanning.
Play with your fancies; and in them behold
Upon the hempen tackle shipboys climbing;
Hear the shrill whistle, which doth order give
To sounds confus'd; behold the threaden sails, 10
Borne with th' invisible and creeping wind,
Draw the huge bottoms through the furrowed sea,
Breasting the lofty surge. O, do but think
You stand upon the rivage and behold
A city on th' inconstant billows dancing; 15
For so appears this fleet majestical,
Holding due course to Harfleur. Follow, follow!
Grapple your minds to sternage of this navy,
And leave your England as dead midnight still,
Guarded with grandsires, babies, and old women, 20
Either past or not arriv'd to pith and puissance;

III. CHORUS. 1 *imagin'd wing* the wing of imagination.   4 *well-appointed* well-
equipped. *Hampton* Southampton (THEOBALD; F¹: "Dover").   5 *brave* fine, gallant,
handsome.   6 *the young Phœbus fanning* fluttering against the rising sun.
fanning ROWE; F¹: "fayning." 7 *Play with your fancies* let your imagination act the
play [K].   10 *threaden* made of thread (linen).   12 *bottoms* ships.   14 *rivage*
shores.   17 *Harfleur* a town at the mouth of the Seine river (F¹, K: "Harflew,"
here and elsewhere).   18 *Grapple . . . navy* let your minds fix themselves to the
sterns of these ships (and follow in their wakes to France).   21 *pith* strength.

For who is he whose chin is but enrich'd
With one appearing hair that will not follow
These _cull'd_ and choice-drawn cavaliers to France?
Work, work your thoughts, and therein see a siege.   25
Behold the _ordinance_ on their carriages,
With fatal mouths gaping on _girded_ Harfleur.
Suppose th' ambassador from the French comes back;
Tells Harry that the King doth offer him
Katherine his daughter, and with her to dowry   30
Some petty and unprofitable dukedoms.
The offer _likes_ not; and the nimble gunner
With _linstock_ now the devilish cannon touches.

                          Alarum, and chambers go off.

And down goes all before them. Still be kind,
And _eke out_ our performance with your mind.   _Exit._

◇◇◇◇◇◇◇◇◇◇◇◇◇◇◇◇◇   ·

[SCENE I. _France. Before Harfleur._]

Alarum. Enter the King, Exeter, Bedford, _and_ Gloucester, [_with_ Soldiers _carrying_] _scaling ladders at Har-
fleur._

KING.   Once more unto the breach, dear friends, once more;
         Or close the wall up with our English dead!
         In peace there's nothing so becomes a man
         As modest stillness and humility;
         But when the blast of war blows in our ears,   5

---

24 _cull'd_ selected.   26 _ordinance_ ordnance.   27 _girded_ besieged, surrounded by men.   32 _likes_ pleases.   33 _linstock_ the match, a bundle of combustibles on the end of a staff, with which old-fashioned cannon were set off [K].   35 _eke out_ supplement (F¹: "eech out").

III.I. 7 _summon_ ROWE; F¹: "commune." Some editors would read "conjure," a plausible emendation.   8 _fair nature_ your naturally humane appearance. _hard-favour'd_ grim-faced.   10 _portage_ portholes (the eyeholes).   11 _o'erwhelm_ over-hang. The action described is that of collecting the eyebrows and causing them to jut out in a terrific frown or scowl [K].   12 _galled_ worn away (by the waves).   13 _jutty_ jut out over. _confounded_ beaten by the sea; or, perhaps, submerged, swallowed up [K].   14 _Swill'd_ wasted, greedily swallowed up. _wasteful_ destructive.

Then imitate the action of the tiger:
Stiffen the sinews, summon up the blood,
Disguise fair nature with hard-favour'd rage;
Then lend the eye a terrible aspect;
Let it pry through the portage of the head   10
Like the brass cannon; let the brow o'erwhelm it
As fearfully as doth a galled rock
O'erhang and jutty his confounded base,
Swill'd with the wild and wasteful ocean.
Now set the teeth and stretch the nostril wide,   15
Hold hard the breath and bend up every spirit
To his full height! On, on, you noblest English,
Whose blood is fet from fathers of war-proof!
Fathers that like so many Alexanders
Have in these parts from morn till even fought,   20
And sheath'd their swords for lack of argument.
Dishonour not your mothers; now attest
That those whom you call'd fathers did beget you!
Be copy now to men of grosser blood
And teach them how to war! And you, good yeomen,   25
Whose limbs were made in England, show us here
The mettle of your pasture. Let us swear
That you are worth your breeding; which I doubt not,
For there is none of you so mean and base
That hath not noble lustre in your eyes.   30
I see you stand like greyhounds in the slips,
Straining upon the start. The game's afoot!
Follow your spirit; and upon this charge
Cry "God for Harry! England and Saint George!"

         [*Exeunt.*] *Alarum, and chambers go off.*

16–17 *bend up . . . full height* stretch every energy to its utmost power. The figure is from bending a bow or from winding up an engine of war (like a catapult or ballista) till it is on the stretch and ready to be discharged [ᴋ].   17 *noblest* F²; F¹: "Noblish"; ᴋ: "noble."   18 *fet* fetched, derived. *of war-proof* whose valour has been tested in war.   19 *Alexanders* Alexander the Great had wept for lack of further worlds to conquer.   21 *argument* subject matter; and so, something to fight about (here practically equal to "opposition") [ᴋ].   24 *Be copy* serve as examples. *men* F⁴; F¹: "me."   25 *yeoman* country men who owned land but were below the rank of gentleman. These comprised the bulk of the English archers. 27 *mettle of your pasture* quality of your rearing.   31 *slips* leashes.   32 *Straining* ʀᴏᴡᴇ; F¹: "Straying."

◇◇◇◇◇◇◇◇◇◇◇◇◇◇◇◇

[SCENE II. *Before Harfleur.*]

Enter Nym, Bardolph, Pistol, *and* Boy.

BARD.   On, on, on, on, on! to the breach, to the breach!

NYM.   Pray thee, Corporal, stay. The knocks are too hot; and,
        for mine own part, I have not a case of lives. The
        humour of it is too hot; that is the very plain-song of it.

PIST.   The plain-song is most just; for humours do abound.   5
            Knocks go and come; God's vassals drop and die;
                And sword and shield
                In bloody field
                Doth win immortal fame.

BOY.   Would I were in an alehouse in London! I would give   10
        all my fame for a pot of ale and safety.

PIST.   And I:
                If wishes would prevail with me,
                My purpose should not fail with me,
                But thither would I hie.   15

BOY.   As duly, but not as truly,
                As bird doth sing on bough.

                Enter Fluellen.

FLU.   Up to the breach, you dogs! Avaunt, you cullions!

                                    [*Drives them forward.*]

III.II. 3 *case of lives* whole set of lives (rather than merely one).   4 *plain-song*
the simple truth. "Plain-song" in music is the simple melody without variations
or the like [K].   5 *just* correct. *humours* Used very inexactly, in Pistol's fashion.
He means that there are many "queer things" happening [K].   16 *As duly . . .
truly* i.e. you would hasten to London "duly" (as surely), but in so doing you would
not be acting "truly" (as becomes a faithful subject) [K]. "Truly" also means "in
tune."   18 *cullions* vile creatures.   19 *men of mould* men of earth, mortal men.
22 *bawcock* fine fellow (from the French "beau coq"). A term of endearment, used
only to men.   *chuck* Another similar term, but of common gender. The absurdity
of Pistol's applying these pet names to the fiery little Welshman who is driving
him into the thick of the fight is obvious [K].   23 *These be good humours* i.e. my
friend Pistol has the right idea [K]. *wins bad humours* i.e. acts in an unpleasant

PIST.   Be merciful, great duke, to men of mould!
Abate thy rage, abate thy manly rage,   20
Abate thy rage, great duke!
Good bawcock, bate thy rage! Use lenity, sweet chuck!

NYM.   These be good humours. Your honour wins bad humours.

Exeunt [all but Boy].

BOY.   As young as I am, I have observ'd these three swashers.
I am boy to them all three; but all they three, though   25
they would serve me, could not be man to me; for
indeed three such antics do not amount to a man. For
Bardolph, he is white-liver'd and red-fac'd; by the
means whereof 'a faces it out, but fights not. For Pistol,
he hath a killing tongue and a quiet sword; by the   30
means whereof 'a breaks words and keeps whole weap-
ons. For Nym, he hath heard that men of few words are
the best men, and therefore he scorns to say his prayers,
lest 'a should be thought a coward; but his few bad
words are match'd with as few good deeds, for 'a never   35
broke any man's head but his own, and that was
against a post when he was drunk. They will steal
anything, and call it purchase. Bardolph stole a lute-
case, bore it twelve leagues, and sold it for three half-
pence. Nym and Bardolph are sworn brothers in filch-   40
ing, and in Calais they stole a fire-shovel. I knew by
that piece of service the men would carry coals. They
would have me as familiar with men's pockets as their
gloves or their handkerchers; which makes much against
my manhood, if I should take from another's pocket to   45

---

way. With Nym "humour" means anything and everything [K].   24 *swashers*
swaggerers, swashbucklers.   25 *boy to* (a) younger than (b) a servant to.   26 *serve*
me be my servants.   *man to me* (a) men in comparison to me (b) servants to me
of any value.   27 *antics* buffoons.   *For* as for.   28 *white-liver'd* cowardly, without
blood in his liver.   29 *'a faces it out* he puts on a bold front.   31 *breaks words*
(a) exchanges words rather than blows (b) uses the language improperly.   33 *best*
most courageous.   36 *broke* To "break one's head" is to draw blood on it — not,
of course, to fracture one's skull [K].   38 *purchase* loot, booty (thieves' slang).
42 *piece of service* (a) warlike exploit (b) bit of thievery.   *carry coals* a slang
phrase for "put up with insults or affronts." Porters who carried coals were
regarded as very low indeed; hence the contemptuous use of the phrase [K].

put into mine; for it is plain <u>pocketing up of wrongs</u>.
I must leave them and seek some better service. Their
villainy <u>goes against my weak stomach</u>, and therefore
I must <u>cast it up</u>.   *Exit.*

Enter Gower [*and* Fluellen].

GOW.   Captain Fluellen, you must come <u>presently</u> to the <u>mines.</u>   50
The Duke of Gloucester would speak with you.

FLU.   To the mines? Tell you the Duke, it is not so good to
come to the mines; for look you, the mines is not
according to the <u>disciplines of the war</u>. The concavities
of it is not sufficient; for look you, th' athversary, you   55
may <u>discuss unto</u> the Duke, look you, is digt himself
four yard under the countermines. By <u>Cheshu</u>, I think
'a will <u>plow</u> up all, if there is not better <u>directions.</u>

GOW.   The Duke of Gloucester, to whom the <u>order</u> of the
siege is given, is altogether directed by an Irishman, a   60
very valiant gentleman, i' faith.

FLU.   It is Captain Macmorris, is it not?

GOW.   I think it be.

FLU.   By Cheshu, he is an ass, as in the world! I will verify
as much in his beard. He has no more directions in the   65
true disciplines of the wars, look you, of the <u>Roman</u>
disciplines, than is a puppy-dog.

Enter Macmorris *and* Captain Jamy.

GOW.   Here 'a comes, and the Scots captain, Captain Jamy,
with him.

FLU.   Captain Jamy is a marvellous <u>falorous</u> gentleman, that   70

---

46 *pocketing up . . . wrongs* (a) putting stolen goods in one's own pocket (b)
putting up with insults — a common expression.   48 *goes . . . stomach* (a) goes
against my inclination (b) makes me sick.   49 *cast it up* (a) give up their service
(b) vomit it up.   50 *presently* immediately. *mines* These were dug under
the walls of the enemy, so as to "undermine" them.   54 *disciplines of the war*
principles of military science. Fluellen's hobby is Roman military theory [K].
Many books on the subject were current in Shakespeare's England.   55–7 *th'
athversary . . . countermines* the enemy has dug counter-mines four yards under
the mines. *discuss unto* inform.   57 *Cheshu* Jesu.   58 *plow* blow. *directions*
management.   59 *order* conduct.   66 *Roman* emphatic. Fluellen's idea is that
only the Romans knew anything about military science. The subject is a mere fad
(or "humour") with him: he is not really a military antiquarian [K].   70 *falorous*

is certain, and of great _expedition_ and knowledge in
th' _aunchiant_ wars, upon my particular knowledge of
his directions. By Cheshu, he will maintain his argument
as well as any military man in the world in the disciplines of the _pristine_ wars of the Romans.   75

JAMY.   I say gud day, Captain Fluellen.

FLU.   _God-den_ to your worship, good Captain James.

GOW.   How now, Captain Macmorris? Have you quit the
         mines? Have the _pioners given o'er_?

MAC.   _By Chrish_, la, tish ill done! The work ish give over, 80
         the trompet sound the retreat. By my hand I swear, and
         my father's soul, the work ish ill done! It ish give over.
         I would have blowed up the town, so Chrish save me
         la! in an hour. O, tish ill done! tish ill done! By my
         hand, tish ill done!   85

FLU.   Captain Macmorris, I beseech you now, will you vout-
         safe me, look you, _a few disputations_ with you, as
         partly touching or concerning the disciplines of the
         war, the Roman wars? In the way of argument, look
         you, and friendly communication; partly to satisfy my 90
         opinion, and partly for the satisfaction, look you, of
         my mind — as touching the direction of the military
         discipline, that is the point.

JAMY.   It sall be vary gud, gud feith, gud Captens bath, and
         I sall _quit_ you with gud leve, as I may _pick occasion_. 95
         That sall I, mary.

MAC.   It is no time to discourse, so Chrish save me! The day
         is hot, and the weather, and the wars, and the King, and

---

valorous. Fluellen confuses his "f" and "v" as well as his "p" and "b." In the
speech of Fluellen, Macmorris, and Jamy, Shakespeare attempts to approximate
the Welsh, Irish, and Scottish dialects.   71 _expedition_ readiness (in battle).
72 _aunchiant_ ancient — of the Romans.   72–3 _upon . . . directions_ I say this on
the basis of my personal knowledge of his management [K].   75 _pristine_ ancient.
77 _God-den_ good e'en — good evening (the regular greeting in the afternoon) [K].
79 _pioners_ diggers, miners. _given o'er_ given up the job.   80 _By Chrish_ by Christ.
Captain Macmorris's brogue is that of the Elizabethan stage Irishman. Doubtless
it was close to nature as is the case with the stage brogue today, but no closer. [K].
87 _a few disputations_ a short discussion.   95 _quit_ repay, answer. _pick occasion_
find opportunity.

the Dukes. It is no time to discourse. The town is <u>be-</u>
<u>seech'd</u>, and the trompet call us to the breach, and we 100
talk, and, be Chrish, do nothing. 'Tis shame for us all.
So God sa' me, 'tis shame to stand still, it is shame, by
my hand! and there is throats to be cut, and works to
be done, and there ish nothing done, so Chrish sa' me, la!

JAMY.   By the mess, ere theise eyes of mine take themselves to 105
slomber, ay'll de gud service, or ay'll lig i' th' grund for
it! ay, or go to death! And ay'll pay't as valorously as
I may, that sall I suerly do, that is the breff and the
long. Mary, I wad full <u>fain heard some question</u> 'tween
you tway.   110

FLU.   Captain Macmorris, I think, look you, under your
correction, there is not many of your nation —

MAC.   <u>Of my nation</u>? What ish my nation? Ish a villain, and
a basterd, and a knave, and a rascal. What ish my
nation? Who talks of my nation?   115

FLU.   <u>Look you</u>, if you take the matter otherwise than is
meant, Captain Macmorris, .peradventure I shall think
you do not <u>use</u> me with that affability as in discretion
you ought to use me, look you, being as good a man
as yourself, both in the disciplines of war, and in the 120
derivation of my birth, and in other particularities.

MAC.   I do not know you so good a man as myself. So Chrish
save me, I will cut off your head!

GOW.   Gentlemen both, <u>you will mistake each other</u>.

JAMY.   Ah, that's a <u>foul fault</u>!   *A parley [sounded].* 125

GOW.   The town sounds a parley.

99–100 *beseech'd* besieged.   109 *fain heard some question* gladly have listened
to some conversation.   111–12 *under your correction* you will correct me if I
am mistaken (a courteous expression).   113 *Of my nation* Macmorris is quick to
suspect that Fleullen means to cast a slur on the Irish [K].   116 *Look you* Fluellen
keeps his temper with difficulty and grows very formal in the process [K].
117 *peradventure* perhaps.   118 *use* treat.   124 *you will . . . other* you insist
on taking each other's words in an offensive sense when no offence is meant [K].
125 *foul fault* bad error in logic [K].   128 *to be required* to be found. He probably
means "acquired."

   III.III. 2 *latest parle* last conference. Contemporary military law provided that

FLU.   Captain Macmorris, when there is more better opportunity to be required, look you, I will be so bold as
to tell you I know the disciplines of war; and there is
an end.   *Exeunt.* 130

◇◇◇◇◇◇◇◇◇◇◇◇◇◇◇◇◇

[SCENE III. *Before the gates of Harfleur.*]

[*Enter the* Governor *and some* Citizens *on the walls.*]
        Enter King [Henry] *and all his* Train *before the
        gates.*

KING.   How yet resolves the Governor of the town?
This is the latest parle we will admit.
Therefore to our best mercy give yourselves,
Or, like to men proud of destruction,
Defy us to our worst; for, as I am a soldier,   5
A name that in my thoughts becomes me best,
If I begin the batt'ry once again,
I will not leave the half-achieved Harfleur
Till in her ashes she lie buried.
The gates of mercy shall be all shut up,   10
And the flesh'd soldier, rough and hard of heart,
In liberty of bloody hand shall range
With conscience wide as hell, mowing like grass }
Your fresh fair virgins and your flow'ring infants.
What is it then to me if impious war,   15
Array'd in flames like to the prince of fiends,
Do with his smirch'd complexion all fell feats
Enlink'd to waste and desolation?

in every siege there was a point after which no real surrender was possible and
that the city would be sacked whether its defenders laid down their arms or not.
King Henry is informing the citizens on the walls that this point has been reached.
admit allow.   4 *proud of destruction* proudly bent on bringing destruction upon
yourselves [K].   8 *half-achieved* only partly conquered.   11 *flesh'd* made fierce by
carnage.   12–13 *In liberty . . . as hell* permitted to engage in slaughter as freely
as he pleases, shall be let loose with a conscience so extended as to permit him to
perform any hellish deed. The victorious soldiers will have the rights of unre-
strained violence and plunder.   17 *smirch'd* blackened with smoke. *fell* cruel.
18 *Enlink'd to* associated with.

What is't to me, when you yourselves are cause,
If your pure maidens fall into the hand   20
Of hot and forcing violation?
What rein can hold licentious wickedness
When down the hill he holds his fierce career?
We may as bootless spend our vain command
Upon th' enraged soldiers in their spoil   25
As send precepts to the Leviathan
To come ashore. Therefore, you men of Harfleur,
Take pity of your town and of your people
Whiles yet my soldiers are in my command,
Whiles yet the cool and temperate wind of grace   30
O'erblows the filthy and contagious clouds
Of heady murder, spoil, and villainy.
If not — why, in a moment look to see
The blind and bloody soldier with foul hand
Defile the locks of your shrill-shrieking daughters;   35
Your fathers taken by the silver beards,
And their most reverend heads dash'd to the walls;
Your naked infants spitted upon pikes,
Whiles the mad mothers with their howls confus'd
Do break the clouds, as did the wives of Jewry   40
At Herod's bloody-hunting slaughtermen.
What say you? Will you yield, and this avoid?
Or, guilty in defence, be thus destroy'd?

GOV.   Our expectation hath this day an end.
The Dauphin, whom of succours we entreated,   45
Returns us that his powers are yet not ready
To raise so great a siege. Therefore, great king,
We yield our town and lives to thy soft mercy.
Enter our gates, dispose of us and ours,
For we no longer are defensible.   [*Exit* Governor.]   50

---

23 *career* headlong course.   24 *bootless* vainly.   25 *in their spoil* while they are
plundering.   26 *precepts* instructions in writing.   31 *O'erblows* blows away.
filthy and contagious clouds Contagion was thought to reside in fog and mists.
The figure is eminently fitting, since one soldier "catches" the spirit of riot and
butchery from another until the whole army is infected [K].   32 *heady* headstrong,
impetuous (F³; F¹: "headly").   34 *blind* reckless.   35 *Defile* ROWE; F¹: "Desire."
40–1 *the wives . . . slaughtermen* cf. MATTHEW, II, 16–18. The lamentations of the

KING. Open your gates. Come, uncle Exeter,
Go you and enter Harfleur; there remain
And fortify it strongly 'gainst the French.
Use mercy to them all. For us, dear uncle,
The winter coming on, and sickness growing   55
Upon our soldiers, we will retire to Calais.
To-night in Harfleur will we be your guest;
To-morrow for the march are we addrest.

Flourish, and enter the town.

❖❖❖❖❖❖❖❖❖❖❖❖❖❖

[SCENE IV. *Rouen. The* French King's *Palace.*]

Enter Katherine *and* [Alice,] *an old* Gentlewoman.

KATH. Alice, tu as esté en Angleterre, et tu parles bien le langage.

ALICE. Un peu, madame.

KATH. Je te prie m'enseignez; il faut que j'apprenne à parler. Comment appelez-vous la main en Anglois?   5

ALICE. La main? Elle est appelée "de hand."

KATH. "De hand." Et les doigts?

ALICE. Les doigts? Ma foi, j'oublie les doigts; mais je me souviendrai. Les doigts? Je pense qu'ils sont appelés "de fingres," oui, "de fingres."   10

KATH. La main, "de hand"; les doigts, "de fingres." Je pense que je suis le bon escolier; j'ai gagné deux mots d'Anglois vistement. Comment appelez-vous les ongles?

ALICE. Les ongles? Nous les appelons "de nails."

---

mothers of the slaughtered innocents were proverbial.   46 *powers* forces, troops.
47 *great* F¹; Q¹, K: "dread."   50 *defensible* capable of defending ourselves.   54 *For us* as for me.   58 *addrest* prepared, ready.

   III.IV. No attempt has been made to record any except the most important of the very numerous corrections and emendations in this scene [K].   1 *parles bien* K; F¹: "bien parlas."   14 *Nous* K; not in F¹.

KATH.   "De nails." Escoutez; dites-moi, si je parle bien: "de   15
        hand, de fingres," et "de nails."

ALICE. C'est bien dict, madame; il est fort bon Anglois.

KATH.   Dites-moi l'Anglois pour le bras.

ALICE. "De arm," madame.

KATH.   Et le coude.   20

ALICE   "D' elbow."

KATH.   "D' elbow." Je m'en fais la répétition de tous les mots
        que vous m'avez appris dès à présent.

ALICE. Il est trop difficile, madame, comme je pense.

KATH.   Excusez-moi, Alice; escoutez: "d' hand, de fingres, de   25
        nails, d' arma, de bilbow."

ALICE. "D' elbow," madame.

KATH.   O Seigneur Dieu, je m'en oublie! "D' elbow." Comment
        appelez-vous le col?

ALICE. "De nick," madame.   30

KATH.   "De nick." Et le menton?

ALICE. "De chin."

KATH.   "De sin." Le col, "de nick"; le menton, "de sin."

ALICE. Oui. <u>Sauf</u> vostre honneur, en vérité, vous prononcez les
        mots aussi droit que les natifs d'Angleterre.   35

KATH.   Je ne doute point d'apprendre, par la grace de Dieu,
        et en peu de temps.

ALICE. <u>N'avez-vous pas déjà</u> oublié ce que je vous ai enseigné?

KATH.   Non, je réciterai à vous promptement: "d' hand, de
        fingres, de <u>mails</u>" —   40

ALICE. "De nails," madame.

---

34 *Sauf* K: F¹: "Sans."   38 *N'avez-vous pas déjà* K: F¹: "N'aue vos y desia."   40 *mails* K; F¹: "Maylees."   47 *De foot et de coun* Since the French equivalents of these sounds are gross obscenities, Katherine's reluctance to repeat these words "devant les seigneurs de France" may be understandable.

   III.v.sd. KITTREDGE, following Q¹ and THEOBALD, gives the speeches beginning at lines 10 and 32 to "Bourbon" and lists him rather than "Bretagne" in this opening stage direction. F¹ gives the speeches to "Brit," clearly the Duke of Bretagne who

KATH.   "De nails, de arm, de ilbow."

ALICE.   Sauf vostre honneur, "d' elbow."

KATH.   Ainsi dis-je; "d' elbow, de nick," et "de sin." Comment
appelez-vous le pied et la robe?   45

ALICE.   "De foot," madame; et "de coun."

KATH.   "De foot et de coun!" O Seigneur Dieu! ce sont mots
de son mauvais, corruptible, gros, et impudique, et non
pour les dames d'honneur d'user: je ne voudrois
prononcer ces mots devant les seigneurs de France pour   50
tout le monde. Foh! "le foot" et "le coun"! Néantmoins, je réciterai une autre fois ma leçon ensemble:
"d' hand, de fingres, de nails, d' arm, d' elbow, de nick,
de sin, de foot, de coun."

ALICE.   Excellent, madame!   55

KATH.   C'est assez pour une fois: allons-nous à diner.   *Exeunt.*

◇◇◇◇◇◇◇◇◇◇◇◇◇◇◇◇◇

[SCENE V. *Rouen. The Palace.*]

Enter the King of France, *the* Dauphin, [Bretagne], *the*
Constable of France, *and others.*

KING.   'Tis certain he hath pass'd the river Somme.

CON.   And if he be not fought withal, my lord,
Let us not live in France; let us quit all
And give our vineyards to a barbarous people.

DAU.   O Dieu vivant! Shall a few sprays of us,   5
The emptying of our fathers' luxury,
Our scions, put in wild and savage stock,

---

is mentioned in Holinshed as among the French King's council, whereas Bourbon
is not.   2 *withal* with.   5 *sprays* offshoots — bastards.   6 *emptying . . . luxury*
the mere dregs of the lust of our ancestors. He is suggesting that the English are
the bastard offspring of the Norman invaders of Britain.   7 *scions . . . stock*
The image is that of the grafting of trees; the "scion" is the "shoot" and the
"stock" the parent stem to which it is grafted.

Spirt up so suddenly into the clouds
And overlook their grafters?

BRET.   Normans, but bastard Normans, Norman bastards!   10
Mort de ma vie! if they march along
Unfought withal, but I will sell my dukedom
To buy a slobb'ry and a dirty farm
In that nook-shotten isle of Albion.

CON.   Dieu de batailles! whence have they this mettle?   15
Is not their climate foggy, raw, and dull,
On whom, as in despite, the sun looks pale,
Killing their fruit with frowns? Can sodden water,
A drench for sur-rein'd jades, their barley broth,
Decoct their cold blood to such valiant heat?   20
And shall our quick blood, spirited with wine,
Seem frosty? O, for honour of our land,
Let us not hang like roping icicles
Upon our houses' thatch, whiles a more frosty people
Sweat drops of gallant youth in our rich fields —   25
"Poor" we may call them in their native lords!

DAU.   By faith and honour,
Our madams mock at us and plainly say
Our mettle is bred out, and they will give
Their bodies to the lust of English youth   30
To new-store France with bastard warriors.

BRET.   They bid us to the English dancing schools
And teach lavoltas high and swift corantos,
Saying our grace is only in our heels
And that we are most lofty runaways.   35

KING.   Where is Montjoy the herald? Speed him hence;

---

8 *Spirt* sprout.   9 *overlook their grafters* become taller than the original trees
from which the shoots ("scions") were taken.   11 *Mort de ma vie* F²; F¹: "Mort du
ma vie," which some editors would read as "Mort Dieu! Ma vie!"   13 *slobb'ry*
muddy.   14 *nook-shotten* shot, or pushed, off into a corner of the earth. The
French nobles regard England as a remote and barbarous island [K]. Some would
interpret the meaning as "indented, irregular, running into corners."   17 *as in
despite* as if despising them.   18 *sodden* boiled. The Constable refers to the
national English beverage — ale [K].   19 *drench* drink. *sur-rein'd* overreined, exhausted by hard riding. *jades* a contemptuous term for "horses." Ale was often
given to tired horses to refresh them [K].   20 *Decoct* warm.   21 *quick* full of life.
23 *roping* hanging down like ropes [K].   26 *"Poor" . . . lords* "Poor" is used to
correct "rich" — our fields are rich in themselves, but they are poor with regard

Let him greet <u>England</u> with our sharp defiance.
Up, princes! and, with spirit of honour edged,
More sharper than your swords, hie to the field.
Charles Delabreth, High Constable of France,   40
You Dukes of Orleans, Bourbon, and of Berri,
Alençon, Brabant, Bar, and Burgundy;
Jaques Chatillon, Rambures, Vaudemont,
Beaumont, Grandpré, Roussi, and Fauconberg,
Foix, Lestrale, Bouciqualt, and Charolois,   45
High dukes, great princes, barons, lords, and <u>knights</u>,
For your great <u>seats</u> now <u>quit you of</u> great shames.
Bar Harry England, that sweeps through our land
With pennons painted in the blood of Harfleur.
Rush on his host as doth the melted snow   50
Upon the valleys whose low vassal seat
The <u>Alps</u> doth spit and void <u>his</u> rheum upon.
Go down upon him — you have <u>power</u> enough —
And in a captive chariot into <u>Roan</u>
Bring him our prisoner.

CON.   This becomes the great.   55
Sorry am I his numbers are so few,
His soldiers sick and famish'd in their march;
For I am sure, when he shall see our army,
He'll drop his heart into the <u>sink</u> of fear
And, <u>for achievement, offer us his ransom</u>.   60

KING.   Therefore, Lord Constable, haste on Montjoy,
And let him say to England that we send
To know what willing ransom he will give.
Prince Dauphin, you shall stay with us in Roan.

to the character of their owners [K].   *we may call* F²; F¹: "we call."   29 *bred out*
exhausted (by in-breeding).   32 *bid us to* bid us go to.   33 *lavoltas* dances in
which there was much leaping about [K].   *corantos* dances in which there was much
rapid movement over the floor [K].   34 *grace* excellence.   *in our heels* (a) in our
dancing ability (b) in our skill at running away.   35 *lofty* showy, high-mannered.
37 *England* the English king.   44-5 *Fauconberg, Foix* CAPELL; F¹: "Faulconbridge,
Loys."   46 *knights* THEOBALD; F¹: "Kings."   47 *seats* fiefs — in return for which
they were bound to fight for the king [K].   *quit you of* redeem yourselves from
[K].   52 *his* the Alps' (treated as a singular).   53 *power* forces, troops.   54 *Roan*
Rouen.   59 *sink* pit, cesspool.   60 *for achievement . . . ransom* instead of winning anything from us, will offer us ransom to allow him to go home [K].

DAU.   Not so, I do beseech your Majesty.   65

KING.   Be patient, for you shall remain with us.
        Now forth, Lord Constable and princes all,
        And quickly bring us word of England's fall.   *Exeunt.*

◆◇◆◇◆◇◆◇◆◇◆◇◆◇◆

[SCENE VI. *The English camp in Picardy.*]

Enter Captains, *English and Welsh* — Gower *and*
        Fluellen.

GOW.   How now, Captain Fluellen? Come you from the bridge?

FLU.   I assure you there is very excellent services <u>committed</u>
        at the bridge.

GOW.   Is the Duke of Exeter safe?

FLU.   The Duke of Exeter is as <u>magnanimous</u> as Agamemnon,   5
        and a man that I love and honour with my soul, and
        my heart, and my duty, and my <u>life,</u> and my living, and
        my uttermost power. He is not — God be praised and
        plessed! — any hurt in the world, but keeps the pridge
        most valiantly, with excellent <u>discipline.</u> There is an   10
        aunchient lieutenant there at the pridge, I think in my
        very conscience he is as valiant a man as Mark Anthony,
        and he is a man of no <u>estimation</u> in the world, but I did
        see him do as gallant service.

GOW.   What do you call him?   15

FLU.   He is call'd Aunchient Pistol.

GOW.   I know him not.

III.VI. 2 *committed* He means "performed." The bridge in question was one
over the river Ternoise, captured by an English patrol on October 23, 1415, and
crossed by the entire English army on the following day, which was the eve of the
battle of Agincourt.   5 *magnanimous* great-souled, valiant.   7 *life* Q¹; F¹, K:
"live," probably a compositor's anticipation of "living."   10 *discipline* military
science. Fluellen's fondness for military science and for the ancients appears on
every occasion [K].   13 *estimation* reputation.   24 *buxom* Perhaps Pistol means
"sturdy," but it is idle to scrutinize very closely his peculiar use of language [K].
25–7 *Fortune's . . . restless stone* Pistol has combined, in a deliciously inconsistent
fashion, two conceptions of Fortune. In one of these her mutability is figured by

Enter Pistol.

FLU.   Here is the man.

PIST.   Captain, I thee beseech to do me favours.
    The Duke of Exeter doth love thee well.   20

FLU.   Ay, I praise God; and I have merited some love at his
    hands.

PIST.   Bardolph, a soldier firm and sound of heart,
    And of buxom valour, hath by cruel fate,
    And giddy Fortune's furious fickle wheel —   25
    That goddess blind,
    That stands upon the rolling restless stone —

FLU.   By your patience, Aunchient Pistol. Fortune is painted
    plind, with a muffler afore her eyes, to signify to you
    that Fortune is plind; and she is painted also with a   30
    wheel, to signify to you, which is the moral of it, that
    she is turning and inconstant, and mutability, and
    variation; and her foot, look you, is fixed upon a
    spherical stone, which rolls, and rolls, and rolls. In good
    truth, the poet makes a most excellent description of it.   35
    Fortune is an excellent moral.

PIST.   Fortune is Bardolph's foe, and frowns on him;
    For he hath stol'n a pax, and hanged must 'a be —
    A damned death!
    Let gallows gape for dog; let man go free,   40
    And let not hemp his windpipe suffocate.
    But Exeter hath given the doom of death
    For pax of little price.
    Therefore, go speak — the Duke will hear thy voice;

---

a wheel (on which she sometimes rides, as in Dürer's picture, and by which she sometimes sits and keeps it turning); in another she stands upon a rolling stone [K]. **28–34** *By your patience . . . and rolls* Fluellen cannot resist the temptation to read Pistol a little lecture on the emblems of Fortune. He is not worried by the inconsistency of Pistol's combination [K]. **29** *her eyes* Q¹; F¹: "his eyes." **38** *pax* a little tablet, containing a relic, or a picture of Christ, the Virgin, or a saint. The pax was kissed by the priest at the mass, and then was passed about to be kissed by the worshippers. Hence its name — from "the kiss of peace" [K]. **42** *doom* judgment.

	And let not Bardolph's vital thread be cut	45
	With edge of penny cord and vile reproach.	
	Speak, Captain, for his life, and I will thee requite.	
FLU.	Aunchient Pistol, I do partly understand your meaning.	
PIST.	Why then, rejoice therefore!	
FLU.	Certainly, aunchient, it is not a thing to rejoice at;	50
	for if, look you, he were my brother, I would desire	
	the Duke to use his good pleasure and put him to	
	execution; for discipline ought to be used.	
PIST.	Die and be damn'd! and <u>figo</u> for thy friendship!	
FLU.	<u>It is well.</u>	55
PIST.	<u>The fig of Spain!</u> *Exit.*	
FLU.	Very good.	
GOW.	Why, this is an <u>arrant</u> counterfeit rascal! I remember	
	him now — a <u>bawd,</u> a cut-purse.	
FLU.	I'll assure you, 'a utt'red as prave words at the	60
	pridge as you shall see in a summer's day. But it is	
	very well. What he has spoke to me, that is well, I	
	warrant you, when time <u>is serve.</u>	
GOW.	Why, 'tis a <u>gull,</u> a fool, a rogue, that now and then	
	goes to the wars to grace himself, at his return into	65
	London, under the form of a soldier. And such fellows	
	are perfect in the great commanders' names, and they	
	will learn you by rote where services were done: — at	
	such and such a <u>sconce,</u> at such a breach, at such a	
	<u>convoy</u>; who <u>came off bravely,</u> who was shot, who dis-	70
	grac'd, what terms the enemy <u>stood</u> on; and this they	
	<u>con</u> perfectly in the <u>phrase of war</u>, which they <u>trick up</u>	

---

54 *figo* a fig. As Pistol says this, he makes an insulting gesture, known as "making
the fig" [K]. It was made by thrusting the thumb between the first and second
fingers.   55 *It is well* Said with awful calmness, which Pistol is unlucky enough
to mistake for cowardice [K].   56 *The fig of Spain* Pistol repeats the gesture. He
says "the fig of Spain!" since the sign in question was used by Spaniards [K].   58
arrant thorough, out-and-out.   59 *bawd* pander.   63 *is serve* shall serve.   64
gull properly, "dupe"; but often used for "foolish fellow" in general [K].   69 *sconce*
breastwork, fortification.   70 *convoy* the guarding of a provision train [K].   *came
off bravely* acquitted himself with credit.   71 *stood* insisted.   72 *con* learn by
heart. *phrase of war* military jargon. *trick up* adorn.

with new-tuned oaths; and what a beard of the General's
cut and a horrid suit of the camp will do among
foaming bottles and ale-wash'd wits is wonderful to be   75
thought on. But you must learn to know such slanders
of the age, or else you may be marvellously mistook.

FLU.   I tell you what, Captain Gower, I do perceive he is not
the man that he would gladly make show to the world
he is. If I find a hole in his coat, I will tell him my   80
mind. [*Drum within.*] Hark you, the King is coming,
and I must speak with him from the pridge.

> *Drum and colours. Enter the* King
> *and his poor* Soldiers, [*and* Gloucester].

God pless your Majesty!

KING.   How now, Fluellen? Cam'st thou from the bridge?

FLU.   Ay, so please your Majesty. The Duke of Exeter has   85
very gallantly maintain'd the pridge; the French is gone
off, look you, and there is gallant and most prave
passages. Marry, th' athversary was have possession of the
pridge, but he is enforced to retire, and the Duke of
Exeter is master of the pridge. I can tell your Majesty,   90
the Duke is a prave man.

KING.   What men have you lost, Fluellen?

FLU.   The perdition of th' athversary hath been very great,
reasonable great. Marry, for my part, I think the Duke
hath lost never a man but one that is like to be executed   95
for robbing a church — one Bardolph, if your Majesty
know the man. His face is all bubukles and whelks, and
knobs, and flames o' fire, and his lips blows at his nose,

---

73 *new-tuned* newly coined (and thus novel sounding).   73-4 *a beard . . . cut*
a beard trimmed like that of the General. Some have suspected an allusion to the
Earl of Essex, who grew a large beard after his Cadiz expedition; this was imitated
by many of his followers.   74 *horrid . . . camp* horrible battle costume.   76-7
slanders of the age persons who are a disgrace to the times [K].   77 *mistook* As
Fluellen has been in the present case by mistaking Pistol for a brave soldier [K].
80 *find . . . coat* discover something discreditable in his record (and thus have
the chance to expose him).   82 *speak . . . pridge* tell him the news I have brought
from the bridge; or, perhaps, speak concerning the bridge [K].   88 *passages* deeds.
93 *perdition* (a) loss (b) destruction.   97 *bubukles* carbuncles.   *whelks* pimples.

and it is like a coal of fire, sometimes plue and sometimes red; but his <u>nose is executed,</u> and his fire 's out. 100

KING.   <u>We would have all such offenders so cut off</u>. And we
give express charge that in our marches through the
country there be nothing <u>compell'd</u> from the villages,
nothing taken but paid for; none of the French up-
braided or abused in disdainful language; for when 105
<u>lenity</u> and cruelty play for a kingdom, the gentler
gamester is the soonest winner.

Tucket. Enter Montjoy.

MONT.   You know me by my habit.

KING.   Well then, I know thee. What shall I know of thee?

MONT.   My master's mind.   110

KING.   Unfold it.

MONT.   Thus says my king: — Say thou to Harry of England:
Though we seem'd dead, we did but sleep. <u>Advantage</u> is
a better soldier than rashness. Tell him we could have
rebuk'd him at Harfleur, but that we thought not good 115
to <u>bruise</u> an injury till it were full ripe. Now we speak
<u>upon our cue,</u> and our voice is imperial. England
shall repent his folly, see his weakness, and <u>admire</u> our
<u>sufferance.</u> Bid him therefore consider of his ransom,
which must proportion the losses we have borne, the 120
subjects we have lost, the disgrace we have digested;
which in weight to re-answer, his pettiness would bow
under. For our losses, his exchequer is too poor; for th'
effusion of our blood, the <u>muster of his kingdom</u> too
faint a number; and for our disgrace, his own person 125

---

100 *nose is executed* It was customary to slit a man's nose as he stood in the pillory
before being hanged. Presumably this is what has happened to Bardolph.   101 *We
would . . . cut off* The King's ignoring of his former familiarity with Bardolph
is grim testimony to his reformation [K]. Yet no audience can envisage Bardolph's
end without some sense of horror and regret.   103 *compell'd* enforced, stolen.
105–6 *lenity* Q¹; F¹: "Leuitie."   107 sd *Tucket* a series of notes on a trumpet.
108 *my habit* He is wearing the costume of a herald, a sleeveless coat (tabard)
bearing a coat of arms.   113 *Advantage* caution (a considerate waiting for an
advantageous opportunity) [K].   116 *bruise* squeeze. The figure is from the treatment of a boil or the like [K].   117 *upon our cue* now the proper moment has

kneeling at our feet but a weak and worthless satisfaction. To this add defiance; and tell him for conclusion, he hath betrayed his followers, whose condemnation is pronounc'd. So far my king and master; so much
my office.   130

KING.   What is thy name? I know thy <u>quality</u>.

MONT.   Montjoy.

KING.   Thou dost thy office <u>fairly</u>. Turn thee back,
And tell thy king I do not seek him now,
But could be willing to march on to Calais   135
Without <u>impeachment</u>: for, to say the sooth,
Though 'tis no wisdom to confess so much
Unto <u>an enemy of craft and vantage,</u>
My people are with sickness much enfeebled,
My numbers lessen'd, and those few I have,   140
Almost no better than so many French;
Who when they were in health, I tell thee, herald,
I thought upon one pair of English legs
Did march three Frenchmen. Yet forgive me, God,
That I do brag thus! This your air of France   145
Hath blown that vice in me. I must repent.
Go therefore tell thy master here I am;
My ransom is this frail and worthless <u>trunk</u>;
My army but a weak and sickly guard;
Yet, God before, tell him we will come on,   150
Though France himself and such another neighbour
Stand in our way. <u>There's for thy labour</u>, Montjoy.

                              [*Gives a purse.*]

Go bid thy master <u>well advise himself</u>:

---

come for us to speak. A common theatrical figure [K].   118 *admire* wonder at.
119 *sufferance* patience.   122–3 *which in weight . . . under* which to make full
compensation for, his slender means are inadequate.   124 *muster of his kingdom*
whole population of England. "Muster" is practically equivalent to "census" [K].
131 *quality* rank and profession.   133 *fairly* handsomely.   136 *impeachment* hindrance.   138 *an enemy of craft and vantage* a crafty enemy who is stronger than
one's self [K].   148 *trunk* The only ransom he will offer is his own body, which
the French king may have if he can get it [K].   152 *There's for thy labour* He
gives the herald a purse or a jewel [K].   153 *well advise himself* consider his course
of action very carefully.

     If we may pass, we will; if we be hind'red,
     We shall your <u>tawny</u> ground with your red blood   155
     Discolour; and so, Montjoy, fare you well.
     The sum of all our answer is but this:
     We would not seek a battle, as we are,
     Nor, as we are, we say we will not shun it.
     So tell your master.   160

MONT.   I shall deliver so. Thanks to your Highness.   [*Exit.*]

GLOUC.   I hope they will not come upon us now.

KING.   We are in God's hand, brother, not in theirs.
     March to the bridge. It now draws toward night.
     Beyond the river we'll encamp ourselves,   165
     And on to-morrow <u>bid them march away</u>.   *Exeunt.*

❖❖❖❖❖❖❖❖❖❖❖❖❖❖❖❖❖

[SCENE VII. *The French camp, near Agincourt.*]

Enter the Constable of France, *the* Lord Rambures,
     Orleans, Dauphin, *with others.*

CON.   Tut! I have the best armour of the world. Would it
     were day!

ORL.   You have an excellent armour; but let my horse have
     his due.

CON.   It is the best horse of Europe.   5

ORL.   Will it never be morning?

DAU.   My Lord of Orleans, and my Lord High Constable,
     you talk of horse and armour?

---

155 *tawny* yellow.   166 *bid them march away* give orders to our army to march towards Calais [K].

   III.VII This frivolous scene is in accordance with what history tells us of the demeanour of the French on the eve of the battle [K].   12 *pasterns* The pastern is part of a horse's foot between the fetlock and the hoof [K] (F²; F¹: "postures").   13 *as if . . . hairs* i.e. as if he were a tennis ball. These were stuffed with hair.   14 *Pegasus* the flying horse ("cheval volant") of Greek mythology. *chez les narines de feu* with fiery nostrils. *chez* THEOBALD; F¹: "ches"; K: "avec." We have no warrant for so radical a correction of Shakespeare's French.   16–17 *basest horn of his hoof* lowest note which his horny hoof sounds as it strikes the earth [K].

ORL.   You are as well provided of both as any prince in the
        world.   10

DAU.   What a long night is this! I will not change my horse
        with any that treads but on four pasterns. Ça, ha! he
        bounds from the earth, as if his entrails were hairs; le
        cheval volant, the Pegasus, chez les narines de feu! When
        I bestride him, I soar, I am a hawk. He trots the air.   15
        The earth sings when he touches it. The basest horn of
        his hoof is more musical than the pipe of Hermes.

ORL.   He's of the colour of the nutmeg.

DAU.   And of the heat of the ginger. It is a beast for Perseus:
        he is pure air and fire; and the dull elements of earth   20
        and water never appear in him, but only in patient
        stillness while his rider mounts him. He is indeed a
        horse, and all other jades you may call beasts.

CON.   Indeed, my lord, it is a most absolute and excellent
        horse.   25

DAU.   It is the prince of palfreys. His neigh is like the bidding
        of a monarch, and his countenance enforces homage.

ORL.   No more, cousin.

DAU.   Nay, the man hath no wit that cannot, from the rising
        of the lark to the lodging of the lamb, vary deserved   30
        praise on my palfrey. It is a theme as fluent as the sea.
        Turn the sands into eloquent tongues, and my horse is
        argument for them all. 'Tis a subject for a sovereign to
        reason on, and for a sovereign's sovereign to ride on;
        and for the world, familiar to us and unknown, to lay   35
        apart their particular functions and wonder at him. I

17 *Hermes* credited with the invention of the pipe.   19 *Perseus* Although some
Greek legends name Bellerophon as the rider of Pegasus, others say that the horse
sprang from the blood of the Gorgon Medusa, slain by Perseus, who rode it when
he rescued Andromeda from the dragon.   26 *palfreys* saddle horses, usually ridden
by ladies and certainly not used in battle. The implication seems to be that the
effeminate Dauphin is riding such a horse.   28 *No more* Orleans is bored by the
Dauphin's extravagant boasting [K].   30 *lodging* lying down to sleep.   30-1 *vary
deserved praise* utter praise in many variations, all of it well-deserved [K].   33
argument subject.   34 *reason* discourse.   35 *the world* all of mankind.   36 *particular functions* individual duties and concerns.

once writ a sonnet in his praise and began thus, "Wonder of nature!"

ORL.   I have heard a sonnet begin so to one's mistress.

DAU.   Then did they imitate that which I compos'd to my   40
         courser, for my horse is my mistress.

ORL.   Your mistress bears well.

DAU.   Me well, which is the prescript praise and perfection of
         a good and particular mistress.

CON.   Nay, for methought yesterday your mistress shrewdly   45
         shook your back.

DAU.   So perhaps did yours.

CON.   Mine was not bridled.

DAU.   O, then belike she was old and gentle, and you rode
         like a kern of Ireland, your French hose off, and in   50
         your strait strossers.

CON.   You have good judgment in horsemanship.

DAU.   Be warn'd by me then. They that ride so, and ride not
         warily, fall into foul bogs. I had rather have my horse
         to my mistress.   55

CON.   I had as lief have my mistress a jade.

DAU.   I tell thee, Constable, my mistress wears his own hair.

CON.   I could make as true a boast as that, if I had a sow to
         my mistress.

DAU.   "Le chien est retourné à son propre vomissement, et la   60
         truie lavée au bourbier." Thou mak'st use of anything.

CON.   Yet do I not use my horse for my mistress, or any such
         proverb so little kin to the purpose.

---

42 *bears* carries a rider (with a bawdy quibble).   43 *prescript* special and appropriate [K].   44 *particular mistress* woman who has one lover only (as opposed to
a whore who is "common").   50 *kern* light-armed Irish foot soldier.   *French hose*
wide breeches.   51 *strait strossers* tight trousers — bare-legged.   56 *lief* F¹, K:
"live," a common variant.   *jade* (a) inferior horse (b) loose woman.   60–1 *Le
chien . . . bourbier* cf. 2 PETER II, 22: "The dog is turned to his own vomit again;
and the sow that was washed to her wallowing in the mire" [K].   *truie* ROWE; F¹:
"leuye."   68 *my sky* He means that there will be stars enough in the sky of his

RAM.   My Lord Constable, the armour that I saw in your tent
         to-night — are those stars or suns upon it?   65

CON.   Stars, my lord.

DAU.   Some of them will fall to-morrow, I hope.

CON.   And yet <u>my sky</u> shall not want.

DAU.   That may be, for you bear a many superfluously, and
         'twere more honour some were away.   70

CON.   Ev'n as your horse bears your praises, who would trot
         as well, were some of your brags <u>dismounted</u>.

DAU.   Would I were able to load him with his desert! Will
         it never be day? I will trot to-morrow a mile, and my
         way shall be paved with English faces.   75

CON.   I will not say so, for fear I should be/fac'd out of my⟩
         way;/but I would it were morning, for I would fain be ⟩
         about the ears of the English.

RAM.   Who will <u>go to hazard with me for twenty prisoners</u>?

CON.   You must first <u>go yourself to hazard</u> ere you have   80
         them.

DAU.   'Tis midnight; I'll go arm myself.   *Exit.*

ORL.   The Dauphin longs for morning.

RAM.   He longs to eat the English.

CON.   I think he will eat all he kills.   85

ORL.   By the white hand of my lady, he's a gallant prince.

CON.   Swear by her foot, that she may <u>tread out the oath</u>.

ORL.   He is simply the most active gentleman of France.

CON.   Doing is activity, and he will still be doing.

ORL.   He never did harm, that I heard of.   90

---

honour [ᴋ].   72 *dismounted* i.e. deflated, taken down a bit.   76–7 *fac'd out of
my way* browbeaten so as to abandon my course. An obvious pun [ᴋ].   79 *go to
hazard . . . prisoners* play at hazard (a game at dice) with twenty English prisoners as the stake [ᴋ].   80 *go yourself to hazard* endure some danger yourself.
87 *tread out the oath* The idea is that the lady may fulfill the oath by dancing,
since the Dauphin is more likely to distinguish himself in that way than in battle
[ᴋ]. To "tread out" also means to "spurn" or to "reject with contempt."

CON.	Nor will do none to-morrow. He will keep that good name <u>still</u>.
ORL.	I know him to be valiant.
CON.	I was told that by one that knows him better than you.
ORL.	What's he? 95
CON.	Marry, he told me so himself, and he said he car'd not who knew it.
ORL.	He needs not; it is no hidden virtue in him.
CON.	By my faith, sir, but it is! Never anybody saw it but <u>his lackey</u>. 'Tis a hooded valour; and when it appears, 100 it will bate.
ORL.	<u>Ill will never said well</u>.
CON.	I will cap that proverb with "There is flattery in friendship."
ORL.	And I will take up that with "Give the devil his due." 105
CON.	Well plac'd! There stands your friend for the devil. Have at the very eye of that proverb with "A pox of the devil!"
ORL.	You are the better at proverbs, by <u>how much</u> "a fool's bolt is soon shot." 110
CON.	You have <u>shot over</u>.
ORL.	'Tis not the first time you were <u>overshot</u>.

Enter a Messenger.

MESS.	My Lord High Constable, the English lie within fifteen hundred paces of your tents.
CON.	Who hath measur'd the ground? 115

---

92 *still* continually.   100 *his lackey* The implication is that only his lackey or servant has ever endured any blows at his hands.   100–1 *hooded valour . . . will bate* The terms are from falconry. His valour is like a hooded falcon which when released will merely flutter his wings (bate). "Bate" also means "abate" or "diminish."   102 *Ill will never said well* The rest of this conversation is an example of the common diversion of "capping proverbs" — answering one proverb by another — the person who has the last word being the winner [K].   109 *how much* as much as.   111 *shot over* overshot the target.   112 *overshot* beaten.   120 *peevish* childish, foolish.   121 *to mope* to come blundering along, like a man walking in his sleep [K].   *fat-brain'd* stupid.   121–2 *so far out of his knowledge*

MESS. The Lord Grandpré.

CON. A valiant and most expert gentleman. Would it were
day! Alas, poor Harry of England! He longs not for the
dawning, as we do.

ORL. What a wretched and <u>peevish</u> fellow is this King of 120
England, <u>to mope</u> with his <u>fat-brain'd</u> followers so far
out of his knowledge!

CON. If the English had any <u>apprehension</u>, they would run
away.

ORL. That they lack; for if their heads had any intellectual 125
armour, they could never wear such heavy headpieces.

RAM. That island of England breeds very valiant creatures.
Their <u>mastiffs are of unmatchable courage.</u>

ORL. Foolish curs, that run <u>winking</u> into the mouth of a
Russian bear and have their heads crush'd like rotten 130
apples! You may as well say that's a valiant flea that
dare eat his breakfast on the lip of a lion.

CON. Just, just! and the men do <u>sympathize with</u> the mastiffs
in <u>robustious</u> and rough <u>coming on,</u> leaving their wits
with their wives; and then give them great meals of 135
beef and iron and steel, they will eat like wolves and
fight like devils.

ORL. Ay, but these English are <u>shrewdly</u> out of beef.

CON. Then shall we find to-morrow they have only <u>stomachs</u>
to eat and none to fight. Now is it time to arm. Come, 140
shall we about it?

ORL. It is now two o'clock; but let me see — by ten
We shall have each a hundred Englishmen.   *Exeunt.*

---

so far away from any region with which he is acquainted. Orleans's comparison is
that of a stupid fellow who blunders into a strange region and loses his way [K].
123 *apprehension* common sense — not "fear." The idea is that they are too stupid
to know the danger they are in [K].   128 *mastiffs . . . courage* The English
mastiffs used in bull and bear baiting, were famous throughout Europe for their
courage and tenacity.   129 *winking* with their eyes closed, oblivious to danger.
133 *sympathize with* resemble.   134 *robustious* boisterous. *coming on* attacking.
138 *shrewdly* cursedly (F¹, K: "shrowdly," a common variant spelling).   139 *stom-
achs* inclinations (with a common pun).

[Act Four]

Chorus.

Now entertain conjecture of a time
When creeping murmur and the poring dark
Fills the wide vessel of the universe.
From camp to camp, through the foul womb of night,
The hum of either army stilly sounds,   5
That the fix'd sentinels almost receive
The secret whispers of each other's watch.
Fire answers fire, and through their paly flames
Each battle sees the other's umber'd face.
Steed threatens steed, in high and boastful neighs   10
Piercing the night's dull ear; and from the tents
The armourers accomplishing the knights,
With busy hammers closing rivets up,
Give dreadful note of preparation.
The country cocks do crow, the clocks do toll   15
And the third hour of drowsy morning name.
Proud of their numbers and secure in soul,
The confident and over-lusty French

IV. CHORUS. 1 *entertain conjecture* receive into your minds an idea. The phrase is practically equivalent to "imagine" [K]. 2 *poring dark* darkness which causes one to pore — strain the eyes in order to see. 3 *wide vessel* empty vault. 4 *foul womb* i.e. because it is black and carries disease, as the night air was believed to do. 5 *stilly sounds* is heard in the stillness. 6 *That* so that. 9 *battle* army. *umber'd* brown or yellowish — on account of the play of firelight on their faces [K]. 12 *accomplishing* finishing — i.e. putting the finishing touches to their armour [K]. 16 *name* TYRWHITT; F¹: "nam'd." 17 *secure* overconfident, free from care. 18 *over-lusty* overmerry. 19 *low-rated* underestimated. *play* play for. 20 *tardy-gaited* slow-stepping. 23 *sacrifices* i.e. to Bellona or Mars, the goddess or god of war. 25 *gesture sad* sober bearing. 26 *Investing* clothing. The figure is a favourite one with Shakespeare. Here the sober bearing of the men is spoken of as clothing their cheeks and coats, inasmuch as one's bearing is in a certain sense the gar-

Do the <u>low-rated</u> English <u>play</u> at dice;
And chide the cripple <u>tardy-gaited</u> night   20
Who like a foul and ugly witch doth limp
So tediously away. The poor condemned English,
Like <u>sacrifices,</u> by their watchful fires
Sit patiently and inly ruminate
The morning's danger; and their <u>gesture sad,</u>   25
<u>Investing</u> lank-lean cheeks and war-worn coats,
<u>Presenteth</u> them unto the gazing moon
So many <u>horrid</u> ghosts. O, now, who will behold
<u>The royal captain</u> of this ruin'd band
Walking from watch to watch, from tent to tent,   30
Let him cry "Praise and glory on his head!"
For forth he goes and visits all his host,
Bids them good morrow with a modest smile
And calls them brothers, friends, and countrymen.
Upon his royal face there is no <u>note</u>   35
How dread an army hath <u>enrounded</u> him;
Nor doth he dedicate one jot of colour⎞
Unto the weary and <u>all-watched night,</u>⎠
But freshly looks, and <u>overbears attaint</u>
With <u>cheerful semblance</u> and sweet majesty;   40
<u>That</u> every wretch, pining and pale before,
Beholding him, plucks comfort from his looks.
A <u>largess universal,</u> like the sun,
His liberal eye doth give to every one,
Thawing cold <u>fear, that</u> <u>mean and gentle all,</u>   45
Behold, <u>as may unworthiness define,</u>

ment which covers everything [K].   27 *Presenteth* HANMER; F¹: "Presented."   28
horrid fearful.   29 *The royal captain* King Henry. Since there is no warrant in
either Hall or Holinshed that Henry visited his men on the eve of Agincourt so
as to cheer them up, this must be taken as Shakespeare's attempt to humanize the
character of the King.   35 *note* indication.   36 *enrounded* surrounded,   37–8
Nor doth . . . night he does not lose any of his freshness of complexion on account
of the fact that he has been awake all night [K].   *all-watched night* the night in
which he has not slept at all [K].   39 *overbears attaint* conquers the natural fagged
appearance which one has who has not slept [K].   40 *cheerful semblance* the appearance of cheerfulness.   41 *That* so that.   43 *largess universal* gift freely given
to all.   45 *fear, that* F¹; THEOBALD, K: "fear. Then." *mean and gentle all* commoners
as well as noblemen.   46 *as may . . . define* so far as our poor and unworthy
abilities can depict it [K].

A little touch of Harry in the night.
And so our scene must to the battle fly;
Where (O for pity!) we shall much disgrace
With four or five most vile and ragged foils,   50
Right ill-dispos'd in brawl ridiculous,
The name of Agincourt. Yet sit and see,
Minding true things by what their mock'ries be.   *Exit.*

◇◇◇◇◇◇◇◇◇◇◇◇◇◇◇◇

[SCENE I.
France. The English camp at Agincourt.]

Enter the King, Bedford, *and* Gloucester.

KING.   Gloucester, 'tis true that we are in great danger;
The greater therefore should our courage be.
Good morrow, brother Bedford. God Almighty!
There is some soul of goodness in things evil,
Would men observingly distil it out;   5
For our bad neighbour makes us early stirrers,
Which is both healthful, and good husbandry.
Besides, they are our outward consciences,
And preachers to us all, admonishing
That we should dress us fairly for our end.   10
Thus may we gather honey from the weed
And make a moral of the devil himself.

Enter Erpingham.

Good morrow, old Sir Thomas Erpingham.

---

47 *A little . . . night* a scene which shall give some slight idea of his conduct as
he goes about the camp [K]. A "touch" is a "glimpse" or "little account."   50 *foils*
persons armed with foils. Properly "foils" were blunted swords used in fencing;
here the term is used contemptuously for the swords which the players carry
[K].   51 *Right ill-dispos'd* very poorly arranged.   52 *Yet* despite the poorness
of our representation [K].   53 *Minding true . . . mock'ries be* seeing in our mind's
eye the actual facts on the basis of the imitations we present [K].

IV.I In the scene that follows — the "little touch of Harry in the night" — the
King has an interview with almost every kind of person in the host. First with a
great noble, Gloucester; next with Sir Thomas Erpingham, a sturdy and honourable old knight; then with the rascally and boasting Pistol; again with Fluellen

A good soft pillow for that good white head
Were better than a <u>churlish</u> turf of France.   15

ERP.   Not so, my liege. This lodging <u>likes</u> me better,
Since I may say "Now lie I like a king."

KING.   'Tis good for men to love their present pains
<u>Upon example:</u> so the spirit is eas'd;
And when the mind is <u>quick'ned</u>, out of doubt   20
The organs, though defunct and dead before,
Break up their drowsy grave and newly move
With <u>casted slough</u> and fresh <u>legerity</u>.
Lend me thy cloak, Sir Thomas. Brothers both,
<u>Commend me</u> to the princes in our camp;   25
<u>Do my good morrow to them</u>, and anon
<u>Desire</u> them all to my <u>pavilion</u>.

GLOUC.   We shall, my liege.

ERP.   Shall I attend your Grace?

KING.   No, my good knight.
Go with my brothers to my lords of England.   30
I and my bosom must debate awhile,
And then I would no other company.

ERP.   The Lord in heaven bless thee, noble Harry!

Exeunt [*all but the* King].

KING.   God-a-mercy, old heart! thou speak'st cheerfully.

Enter Pistol.

PIST.   <u>Qui va là?</u>   35

---

and Gower, two captains equally devoted to him, but of a different race; last of
all, with the sturdy English private soldiers, Bates, who represents the good-na-
tured and easygoing Englishman, and Williams, who is a fine example of the
national habit of grumbling, in which John Bull has always taken a certain
pride [K].   4 *soul* kernel.   5 *observingly* by careful observation.   7 *husbandry*
economy, thrift.   10 *dress us fairly* well prepare ourselves.   15 *churlish* niggardly.   16 *likes* pleases.   19 *Upon example* by considering the example of others.
20 *quick'ned* enlivened.   23 *casted slough* The figure is from a snake which casts
its skin [K].   *legerity* nimbleness, vigour.   25 *Commend me* give my regards.
26 *Do . . . them* say good morning to them in my name.   27 *Desire* request.
pavilion war tent.   35 *Qui va là* who goes there? (ROWE; F¹: "Che vous la").

KING. A friend.

PIST. Discuss unto me, art thou officer;
Or art thou base, common, and <u>popular</u>?

KING. I am a <u>gentleman of a company</u>.

PIST. <u>Trail'st thou the puissant pike</u>?   40

KING. Even so. What are you?

PIST. As good a gentleman as the Emperor.

KING. Then you are a better than the King.

PIST. The King's a <u>bawcock</u>, and a heart of gold,
A lad of life, an <u>imp of fame</u>,   45
Of parents good, of fist most valiant.
I kiss his dirty shoe, and from heartstring
I love the lovely <u>bully</u>. What is thy name?

KING. Harry le Roy.

PIST. Le Roy? A Cornish name. Art thou of Cornish crew?   50

KING. No, I am a Welshman.

PIST. Know'st thou Fluellen?

KING. Yes.

PIST. Tell him I'll knock his leek about his pate
Upon Saint Davy's day.   55

KING. Do not you wear your dagger in your cap that day, lest
he knock that about yours.

PIST. Art thou his friend?

KING. And <u>his kinsman</u> too.

PIST. <u>The figo</u> for thee then!   60

---

38 *popular* of the common people, vulgar.   39 *gentleman of a company* inferior (noncommissioned) officer.   40 *Trail'st . . . pike* are you in the infantry? To "trail" the pike was to carry it with the butt touching the ground.   44 *bawcock* fine fellow ("beau coq").   45 *imp of fame* child of renown.   48 *bully* a slang term of endearment [K].   54–5 *his leek . . . Saint Davy's day* On St. David's Day, March 1, Welshmen still wear a leek to commemorate their victory over the Saxons. *pate* head.   59 *his kinsman* The Welsh were famous for keeping their genealogical connections up to the remotest degree. Hence it is proverbial that all Welsh gentlemen are related [K].   60 *The figo* He makes the sign of the "fig."   63 *sorts well with* befits.   65 *lower* Q³; F¹: "fewer"; Q¹: "lewer."   66 *admiration* wonder.   70

KING.   I thank you. God be with you!

PIST.   My name is Pistol call'd.   *Exit. Manet* King.

KING.   It <u>sorts well with</u> your fierceness.

Enter Fluellen *and* Gower.

GOW.   Captain Fluellen!

FLU.   So! in the name of Jesu Christ, speak <u>lower</u>, It is the   65
          greatest <u>admiration</u> in the universal world, when the true
          and aunchient prerogatifes and laws of the wars is not
          kept. If you would take the pains but to examine the
          wars of Pompey the Great, you shall find, I warrant you,
          that there is no <u>tiddle taddle</u> nor <u>pibble pabble</u> in Pom-   70
          pey's camp/I warrant you, you shall find the ceremonies
          of the wars, and the cares of it, and the forms of it, and
          the sobriety of it, and the <u>modesty</u> of it, to be otherwise.

GOW.   Why, the enemy is loud; you hear him all night.

FLU.   If the enemy is an ass and a fool and a prating coxcomb,   75
          is it <u>meet</u>, think you, that we should also, look you, be an
          ass and a fool and a prating coxcomb? In your own con-
          science now?

GOW.   <u>I will speak lower</u>.

FLU.   I pray you and beseech you that you will.   80

Exeunt [Gower *and* Fluellen].

KING.   Though it appear a little <u>out of fashion,</u>
          There is much <u>care</u> and valour in this Welshman.

Enter three Soldiers, John Bates, Alexander Court, *and* Michael Williams.

---

tiddle taddle title tattle. *pibble pabble* bibble babble. Both terms mean "mean-
ingless chatter."   70–1 *Pompey's camp* Fluellen's example is unfortunate, inasmuch as Pompey's most famous camp, that just before the Battle of Pharsalia, was
noted for its luxury and lack of discipline. No doubt Shakespeare knew this from
Plutarch, and intentionally makes Fluellen's learning go astray [K].   73 *modesty*
moderation.   76 *meet* fitting.   79 *I will speak lower* Gower is convinced of the
wisdom of Fluellen's words [K].   81 *out of fashion* quaint, old-fashioned.   82
care carefulness. Fluellen's valour is well-known. His caution is shown in the
preceding conversation which the King has overheard [K].

COURT.   Brother John Bates, is not that the morning which
          breaks yonder?

BATES.   I think it be; but we have no great cause to desire the   85
          approach of day.

WILL.   We see yonder the beginning of the day, but I think we
          shall never see the end of it. Who goes there?

KING.   A friend.

WILL.   Under what captain serve you?   90

KING.   Under Sir Thomas Erpingham.

WILL.   A good old commander and a most kind gentleman. I
          pray you, what thinks he of our estate?

KING.   Even as men wrack'd upon a sand, that look to be wash'd
          off the next tide.   95

BATES.   He hath not told his thought to the King?

KING.   No; nor it is not meet he should. For thought I speak
          it to you, I think the King is but a man, as I am. The
          violet smells to him as it doth to me; the element shows
          to him as it doth to me; all his senses have but human   100
          conditions. His ceremonies laid by, in his nakedness he
          appears but a man; and though his affections are higher
          mounted than ours, yet, when they stoop, they stoop
          with the like wing. Therefore, when he sees reason of
          fears, as we do, his fears, out of doubt, be of the same 105
          relish as ours are. Yet, in reason, no man should possess
          him with any appearance of fear, lest he, by showing it,
          should dishearten his army.

91 *Thomas* THEOBALD; F¹: "John."   93 *estate* state, condition.   94 *wrack'd* ship-
wrecked. *sand* sand bar.   97 *it is not* F¹; DYCE, K: "is it not."   99 *element shows*
sky appears.   101 *conditions* characters, qualities.   *ceremonies* clothes of state,
splendid apparel [K]; those things in general which are the signs of royalty.   102
affections feelings.   102–3 *are higher mounted* soar higher (a term from falconry).
103 *stoop* descend in flight.   104 *with the like wing* in the same way.   104–5 *of
fears* for fear.   105 *out of doubt* beyond question.   105–6 *be of the same relish*
taste the same way to him — i.e. when the King feels, his feeling is like ours, though
when he hopes, his hopes may be higher than ours [K].   106–7 *no man . . . of
fear* no man should put the King in possession of (i.e. let the King see) any appearance of fear in him [K].   112 *at all adventures* at all hazards. Bates means that he

BATES.   He may show what outward courage he will; but I believe, as cold a night as 'tis, he could wish himself in 110
Thames up to the neck; and so I would he were, and I
by him, at all adventures, so we were quit here.

KING.   By my troth, I will speak my conscience of the King: I
think he would not wish himself anywhere but where
he is.   115

BATES.   Then I would he were here alone. So should he be sure
to be ransomed, and a many poor men's lives saved.

KING.   I dare say you love him not so ill to wish him here alone,
howsoever you speak this to feel other men's minds. Methinks I could not die anywhere so contented as in the 120
King's company, his cause being just and his quarrel
honourable.

WILL.   That's more than we know.

BATES.   Ay, or more than we should seek after; for we know
enough if we know we are the King's subjects. If his 125
cause be wrong, our obedience to the King wipes the
crime of it out of us.

WILL.   But if the cause be not good, the King himself hath a
heavy reckoning to make when all those legs and arms
and heads, chopp'd off in a battle, shall join together at 130
the latter day and cry all "We died at such a place!"
some swearing, some crying for a surgeon, some upon
their wives left poor behind them, some upon the debts
they owe, some upon their children rawly left. I am
afeard there are few die well that die in a battle; for 135

would take the risk of being in the Thames up to the neck rather than the risk of
being in his present situation [K].   *quit here* out of this situation.   113 *conscience*
true thoughts.   121 *his cause being just* The King's confidence in the justice of
his cause is insisted on with good effect here. Our minds revert to the elaborate discussion of this question at the beginning of the play [K].   124–7 *for we know . . .
out of us* Bates here states the official Tudor position in reply to Cardinal William
Allen, who had urged English Catholics to desert Queen Elizabeth on the grounds
that soldiers fighting in an unjust cause damn their own souls and that it is their
duty to rebel against a ruler who commands them to do evil.   131 *latter day* day
of judgment.   134 *rawly left* left in poor circumstances, unprovided for.   135 *die
well* die a Christian death.

how can they <u>charitably dispose of anything</u> when blood
is their <u>argument</u>? Now, if these men do not die well, it
will be a black matter for the King that led them to it;
who to disobey were against <u>all proportion of subjection</u>.

KING.   <u>So</u>, if a son that is by his father <u>sent about merchandise</u> 140
<u>do sinfully miscarry upon the sea</u>, the <u>imputation</u> of his
wickedness, by your rule, should be imposed upon his
father that sent him; or if a servant, under his master's
command transporting a sum of money, be assailed by
robbers and die <u>in many irreconcil'd iniquities</u>, you may 145
call the business of the master the author of the servant's
damnation. But this is not so. The King is not bound to
<u>answer the particular endings of his soldiers</u>, the father
of his son, nor the master of his servant; for <u>they</u> purpose not their death when they purpose their services. 150
Besides, there is no king, be his cause never so spotless,
if it come to the <u>arbitrement of swords</u>, can try it out
with all <u>unspotted</u> soldiers. Some (<u>peradventure</u>) have
on them the guilt of premeditated and contrived murder; some, of beguiling virgins with the broken seals of 155
perjury; some, <u>making the wars their bulwark</u>, that have
before gored the gentle bosom of peace with pillage and
robbery. Now, if these men have defeated the law and
<u>outrun native punishment</u>, though they can outstrip
men, they have no wings to fly from God. War is his 160
<u>beadle</u>, war is his vengeance; so that here men are pun-
ish'd for before-breach of the King's laws in now the

136 *charitably . . . anything* make such a disposition of their affairs as accords
with Christian charity [K].   137 *argument* subject of their thoughts.   139 *all
proportion of subjection* all propriety or reason on the part of his subjects [K].
140 *So* i.e. on the principle that Williams has just laid down. Williams's arguments
are common and would instantly appeal to the rank and file in the Elizabethan
theatre. The King's computation of fame is a good example of his ability to reason
in morality and justifies the opinion pronounced on him by the Archbishop of
Canterbury in the first act [K].   140 *sent about merchandise* sent on a trading
voyage [K].   141 *do sinfully . . . sea* is lost at sea while in a state of sin [K]. *im-
putation of* responsibility for.   145 *in many irreconcil'd iniquities* with many sins
upon his conscience for which he has not made his peace with God [K].   148 *answer
. . . soldiers* be responsible for the particular way in which each of his soldiers
meets his death — i.e. whether in a condition of harmony with God or the reverse
[K].   149 *they* i.e. the king, the father, the master.   152 *arbitrement of swords*

King's quarrel. Where they feared the death, they have
borne life away; and where they would be safe, they
perish. Then if they die <u>unprovided</u>, no more is the 165
King guilty of their damnation than he was before
guilty of those impieties for the which they are now
<u>visited</u>. Every subject's duty is the King's, but every sub-
ject's soul is his own. Therefore should every soldier in
the wars do as every sick man in his bed — wash every 170
.<u>mote</u> out of his conscience; and <u>dying so</u>, death is to him
advantage; or not dying, the time was blessedly lost
wherein such preparation was gained; and in him that
escapes, it were not sin to think that, making God so free
an offer, he let him outlive that day to see his greatness 175
and to teach others how they should prepare.

WILL.   'Tis certain, every man that dies ill, the ill upon his own
head — the King is not to answer it.

BATES.   I do not desire he should answer for me, and yet I determine to fight <u>lustily</u> for him.   180

KING.   I myself heard the King say he would not be ransom'd.

WILL.   Ay, he said so, to make us fight cheerfully; but when our
throats are cut, he may be ransom'd, and we ne'er the
wiser.

KING.   If I live to see it, I will never trust his word after.   185

WILL.   You pay him then! That's a perilous shot out of an elder-
gun, that a poor and a private displeasure can do against
a monarch! You may as well <u>go about</u> to turn the sun
to ice with fanning in his face with a peacock's feather.

---

judgment by battle.   153 *unspotted* unstained by sin.   *peradventure* perhaps.
156 *making . . . bulwark* hiding behind the defence of warfare. Taking advantage,
in other words, of a warlike time, these soldiers have inflicted injury on noncombatants or peaceable citizens [K].   159 *outrun native punishment* escaped punishment in their native land [K].   161 *beadle* an officer whose duty it was to whip
criminals.   165 *unprovided* with souls unprepared for death.   168 *visited* punished.   171 *mote* least spot — a manifest allusion to the parable of the mote and
the beam [K].   *dying so* i.e. dying with a clear conscience.   174-5 *making . . .
offer* since he offered his soul so freely to the Lord [K].   177-8 *'Tis certain . . .
answer it* Williams is convinced by the King's logic and sums up the argument in
complete assent with him [K].   180 *lustily* vigorously.   186-7 *an elder-gun* a pop-
gun made out of an elder stick with the pith taken out [K].   188 *go about* under-
take.

You'll never trust his word after! Come, 'tis a foolish 190
saying.

KING.   Your reproof is <u>something too round</u>. I should be angry
with you if the time were convenient.

WILL.   Let it be a quarrel between us if you live.

KING.   I <u>embrace it</u>.   195

WILL.   How shall I know thee again?

KING.   Give me any <u>gage</u> of thine, and I will wear it in my
<u>bonnet.</u> Then, if ever thou dar'st acknowledge it, I will
make it my quarrel.

WILL.   Here's my glove. Give me another of thine.   200

KING.   There.

WILL.   This will I also wear in my cap. If ever thou come to
me and say, after to-morrow, "This is my glove," by this
hand, I will <u>take</u> thee a box on the ear.

KING.   If ever I live to see it, I will challenge it.   205

WILL.   Thou dar'st as well be hang'd.

KING.   Well, I will do it, though I take thee in the King's
company.

WILL.   Keep thy word. Fare thee well.

BATES. Be friends, you English fools, be friends! We have 210
French quarrels <u>enow</u>, if you could tell how to reckon.

KING.   Indeed the French may <u>lay</u> twenty French crowns to
one they will beat us, for they bear them on their
shoulders; but it is no English treason /to cut French↲

---

192 *something too round* somewhat too blunt.   195 *embrace it* accept your offer.
197 *gage* pledge.   198 *bonnet* cap.   204 *take* give.   211 *enow* enough.   212 *lay*
bet. The pun on "crowns" is obvious.   214–15 *to cut French crowns* The two
senses are (a) to clip the coins known as French crowns (b) to cut French heads
with a sword [K].   215–16 *a clipper* This carries out the pun. A person who cut
off small pieces of coin so as to make them underweight was called a clipper. The
punishment for this was death. It was easy to clip coins in old times, because they
were not exactly round and had not milled edges as at the present day [K].   218
careful anxious, full of care.   221 *subject* This agrees with "greatness." Majesty
itself is subject to the foolish talk of everybody [K]. *breath* words, speech.   222
sense sensibility, sensitiveness.   223 *his own wringing* that which pinches him.
"To wring" was "to pinch" or "to twist." There is doubtless an allusion to the

crowns, and to-morrow the King himself will be a 215
clipper.   *Exeunt* Soldiers.

Upon the King! Let us our lives, our souls,
Our debts, our careful wives,
Our children, and our sins, lay on the King!
We must bear all. O hard condition,   220
Twin-born with greatness, subject to the breath
Of every fool, whose sense no more can feel
But his own wringing! What infinite heart's-ease
Must kings neglect that private men enjoy!
And what have kings that privates have not too,   225
Save ceremony, save general ceremony?
And what art thou, thou idol Ceremony?
What kind of god art thou, that suffer'st more
Of mortal griefs than do thy worshippers?
What are thy rents? What are thy comings-in?   230
O Ceremony, show me but thy worth!
What is thy soul of adoration?
Art thou aught else but place, degree, and form,
Creating awe and fear in other men?
Wherein thou art less happy being fear'd   235
Than they in fearing.
What drink'st thou oft, instead of homage sweet,
But poison'd flattery? O, be sick, great greatness,
And bid thy ceremony give thee cure!
Thinks thou the fiery fever will go out   240
With titles blown from adulation?
Will it give place to flexure and low bending?

old proverb, "I know best myself where my shoe wrings me," or, as we say now,
"where the shoe pinches" [K].   *heart's-ease* contentment.   224 *neglect* disregard,
pass by, do without — not implying any culpability, as is the case today with the
word [K].   226 *ceremony* all the outward shows and appurtenances of kingship.
230 *comings-in* income.   232 *thy soul of adoration* that essential quality which
makes thee so much adored [K].   233 *place, degree, and form* position, rank, and
outward show.   238 *great greatness* The repetition, like plays on words in general,
here expresses contempt [K].   240 *Thinks* A common Elizabethan form (F¹; ROWE,
K: "Think'st").   240–41 *will go out . . . adulation* will be extinguished by the
mere words of flatterers.   241 *blown* Words are but breath, and breath is but
air; hence it is common to find all sorts of words appropriate to wind used of
speech [K].   242 *give place to* yield to, retire before. *flexure* bowing.

Canst thou, when thou command'st the beggar's knee,
Command the health of it? No, <u>thou proud dream,</u>
That <u>play'st so subtilly with a king's repose.</u>   245
I am a king that <u>find thee;</u> and I know
'Tis not the <u>balm,</u> the sceptre, and the ball,
The sword, the mace, the crown imperial,
The <u>intertissued robe of gold and pearl,</u>
The <u>farced</u> title running fore the king,   250
The throne he sits on, nor the <u>tide of pomp</u>
That beats upon the high shore of this world —
No, not all these, thrice-gorgeous ceremony,
Not all these, laid in bed majestical,
Can sleep so soundly as the wretched slave,   255
Who, with a body fill'd, and <u>vacant</u> mind,
Gets him to rest, cramm'd with <u>distressful bread;</u>
Never sees horrid night, the child of hell;
But like <u>a lackey,</u> from the rise to set,
Sweats in the eye of <u>Phœbus,</u> and all night   260
Sleeps in Elysium; next day after dawn,
Doth rise and help <u>Hyperion</u> to his horse;
And follows so the ever-running year
With profitable labour to his grave;
And but for ceremony, such a wretch,   265
<u>Winding up</u> days with toil and nights with sleep,
Had the <u>forehand</u> and vantage of a king.
The slave, a <u>member of the country's peace,</u>
Enjoys <u>it;</u> but in <u>gross</u> brain little <u>wots</u>
What <u>watch</u> the king keeps to maintain the peace,   270

---

244 *thou proud dream* The King is still apostrophizing ceremony [K].   245 *play'st
. . . repose* cheats a king so cleverly out of his repose [K]. The cares of kingship
which prevent the weary ruler from sleeping are a constant Renaissance theme upon
which Shakespeare dwells also in the HENRY IV plays.   246 *find thee* detect thy
real nature.   247 *balm* holy oil with which kings are annointed at their coronation.   249 *intertissued . . . and pearl* coronation mantle interwoven with gold
and pearls [K].   250 *farced* stuffed, unnaturally inflated. The word expresses contempt.   251 *tide of pomp* flood tide of splendid ceremony [K].   256 *vacant* free
from care.   257 *distressful bread* bread gained by hard labour [K].   259 *a lackey*
a servant who runs before the coach of his master.   260 *Phœbus* the sun god.
262 *Hyperion* the sun. In order to help Hyperion harness his horses one must, of
course, rise before dawn [K].   266 *Winding up* occupying and closing [K].   267
forehand advantage.   268 *member . . . peace* citizen of a peaceful community.

Whose hours the peasant best <u>advantages.</u>

Enter Erpingham.

ERP.   My lord, your nobles, <u>jealous of</u> your absence,
        Seek through your camp to find you.

KING.   Good old knight,
        Collect them all together at my tent.
        I'll be before thee.

ERP.   I shall do't, my lord.   *Exit.* 275

KING.   O God of battles, steel my soldiers' hearts,
        Possess them not with fear! Take from them now
        The <u>sense of reck'ning</u>, if th' opposed numbers
        Pluck their hearts from them. Not to-day, O Lord,
        O not to-day, think not upon the fault   280
        My father made in <u>compassing</u> the crown!
        I Richard's body have interred new;
        And on it have bestowed more contrite tears
        Than from it issued forced drops of blood.
        Five hundred poor I have in yearly pay,   285
        Who twice a day their wither'd hands hold up
        Toward heaven, to pardon blood; and I have built
        Two <u>chantries</u>, where the sad and solemn priests
        Sing <u>still</u> for Richard's soul. More will I do!
        Though all that I can <u>do</u> is nothing worth,   290
        Since that my penitence comes after all,
        Imploring pardon.

Enter Gloucester.

---

269 *it* i.e. the peace which the king maintains [K].   *gross* stupid.   *wots* knows.
270 *watch* sleepless nights.   271 *advantages* profits from.   272 *jealous of* concerned about.   278 *sense of reck'ning* ability to count (the numbers of the enemy)
280–1 *not to-day . . . the crown* The King never forgets — and Shakespeare never
permits his audience to forget — that his father was the murderer of Richard II
and a usurper of the crown.   281 *compassing* obtaining.   288 *chantries* chapels
for the performance of special masses for the souls of the dead. They were usually
attached to a cathedral church [K].   289 *still* ever, without ceasing.   290 *do*
Emphatic. He means that no mere actions can expiate the guilt of Richard's
murder, since, when he has done everything that is possible, he feels that he must
still add his penitent prayers to God to forgive his father's crime, the guilt of
which seems in a manner to descend to him [K].

GLOUC.   My liege!

KING.   My brother Gloucester's voice? Ay.
    I know thy errand; I will go with thee.   295
    The day, my <u>friends,</u> and all things stay for me.

                                       Exeunt.

◆◆◆◆◆◆◆◆◆◆◆◆◆◆◆◆◆

[SCENE II. *The French camp.*]

Enter the Dauphin, Orléans, Rambures, *and* Beaumont.

ORL.   The sun doth gild our armour. <u>Up</u>, my lords!

DAU.   Montez à cheval! My horse! Varlet, laquais! Ha!

ORL.   O brave spirit!

DAU.   Via! les eaux et la terre —

ORL.   Rien puis? L'air et le feu.   5

DAU.   <u>Ciel</u>! cousin Orleans.

                Enter Constable.

    Now, my Lord Constable?

CON.   Hark how our steeds for <u>present service</u> neigh!

DAU.   Mount them and make incision in their hides,
    That their hot blood may spin in English eyes   10
    And <u>dout them</u> <u>with superfluous courage,</u> ha!

RAM.   What, will you have them weep our horses' blood?
    How shall we then behold their natural tears?

                Enter Messenger.

---

296 *friends* Q¹; F¹: "friend."

    IV.II. 1 *Up* not "rise from sleep," of course, but "to horse" [K].   6 *Ciel* THEOBALD; F¹: "Cein."   8 *present service* immediate action.   11 *dout them* put them (the eyes) out; do them out. *with superfluous courage* with the blood which they have in greater abundance than is necessary. Courage and fullness of blood were thought to go together. The horses, having a superabundance of courage, may well spare some of their blood [K].   14 *embattail'd* arranged in battle order.   17 *fair show* gallant appearance.   18 *shales* shells.   21 *naked curtleaxe* bared cutlass.

MESS.   The English are embattail'd, you French peers.

CON.   To horse, you gallant princes! straight to horse!   15
    Do but behold yond poor and starved band,
    And your fair show shall suck away their souls,
    Leaving them but the shales and husks of men.
    There is not work enough for all our hands,
    Scarce blood enough in all their sickly veins   20
    To give each naked curtleaxe a stain
    That our French gallants shall to-day draw out
    And sheathe for lack of sport. Let us but blow on them,
    The vapour of our valour will o'erturn them.
    'Tis positive 'gainst all exceptions, lords,   25
    That our superfluous lackeys and our peasants,
    Who in unnecessary action swarm
    About our squares of battle, were enow
    To purge this field of such a hilding foe,
    Though we upon this mountain's basis by   30
    Took stand for idle speculation:
    But that our honours must not. What's to say?
    A very little little let us do,
    And all is done. Then let the trumpets sound
    The tucket sonance and the note to mount;   35
    For our approach shall so much dare the field
    That England shall couch down in fear and yield.

Enter Grandpré.

GRAND.   Why do you stay so long, my lords of France?
    Yond island carrions, desperate of their bones,
    Ill-favouredly become the morning field.   40
    Their ragged curtains poorly are let loose,
    And our air shakes them passing scornfully.

---

25 *'Tis positive 'gainst all exceptions* it may be asserted positively in defiance of all objection or contradiction [K].   28 *enow* enough.   29 *hilding* wretched, insignificant. Used either as a noun or as an adjective [K].   31 *speculation* looking on.   35 *tucket sonance* trumpet call. *note* signal.   36 *dare the field* frighten the enemy.   37 *couch* lie, crouch.   39 *carrions* skeletons. *desperate of* without hope of saving.   40 *Ill-favouredly . . . field* i.e. these scarecrows are a disfigurement to the fair landscape and ought to be cleared away [K].   41 *curtains* banners.   42 *passing* passingly, exceedingly.

Big Mars seems bankrout in their beggar'd host
And faintly through a rusty beaver peeps.
The horsemen sit like fixed candlesticks   45
With torch-staves in their hand; and their poor jades
Lob down their heads, dropping the hides and hips,
The gum down roping from their pale-dead eyes,
And in their pale dull mouths the gimmal'd bit
Lies foul with chaw'd grass, still and motionless;   50
And their executors, the knavish crows,
Fly o'er them, all impatient for their hour.
Description cannot suit itself in words
To demonstrate the life of such a battle
In life so lifeless as it shows itself.   55

CON.   They have said their prayers, and they stay for death.

DAU.   Shall we go send them dinners and fresh suits
And give their fasting horses provender,
And after fight with them?

CON.   I stay but for my guidon. To the field!   60
I will the banner from a trumpet take
And use it for my haste. Come, come away!
The sun is high, and we outwear the day.   *Exeunt.*

❖❖❖❖❖❖❖❖❖❖❖❖❖❖

[SCENE III. *The English camp.*]

Enter Gloucester, Bedford, Exeter, Erpingham *with all
his host,* Salisbury, *and* Westmoreland.

---

43 *Big* threatening. The idea is that they look like a troop of military bankrupts —
so poverty-stricken in their appearance [K]. *bankrout* bankrupt.   44 *beaver*
moveable visor of a helmet.   45 *candlesticks* Ornamental candlesticks, etc., often
had the form of horsemen, lance in hand [K].   46 *jades* inferior horses.   47 *Lob*
hang dejectedly.   48 *down roping* trickling down.   49 *gimmal'd* jointed. A
"gimmal'd bit" consisted of two twin parts hinged together (DELIUS; F¹: "lymold").
51 *executors* those who inherit and dispose of what is left of the dead. The crows
will pick the bones, which will be all that these men and horses can bequeath to
them.   53 *suit itself in words* clothe itself in fitting terms [K].   54 *To demonstrate . . . battle* to describe such an army "to the life." Note the scornful playing
on the word "life" in the next verse [K].   60 *guidon* the pennant or little ban-

GLOUC.   Where is the King?

BED.   The King himself is rode to view their battle.

WEST.   Of fighting men they have full three-score thousand.

EXE.   There's five to one; besides, they all are fresh.

SAL.   God's arm strike with us! 'Tis a fearful odds.   5
        God buy you, princes all; I'll to my charge.
        If we no more meet till we meet in heaven,
        Then joyfully, my noble Lord of Bedford,
        My dear Lord Gloucester, and my good Lord Exeter,
        And my kind kinsman, warriors all, adieu!   10

BED.   Farewell, good Salisbury, and good luck go with thee!

EXE.   Farewell, kind lord. Fight valiantly to-day;
        And yet I do thee wrong to mind thee of it, ⎫
        For thou art fram'd of the firm truth of valour. ⎭

                              [*Exit* Salisbury.]

BED.   He is as full of valour as of kindness,   15
        Princely in both.

                  Enter the King.

WEST.   O that we now had here
        But one ten thousand of those men in England
        That do no work to-day!

KING.   What's he that wishes so?
        My cousin Westmoreland? No, my fair cousin.
        If we are mark'd to die, we are enow ⎫   20
        To do our country loss; and if to live, ⎭

---

ner fixed to a staff — his official sign as commander [K] (RANN; F¹: "Guard. On,"
which has been defended by some editors).   61 *banner* streamer affixed to a
trumpet. *trumpet* trumpeter.   63 *outwear* waste in idleness [K].
    IV.III. 2 *battle* army drawn up in formation.   6 *God buy you* A common ex-
pression combining the senses of "God be with you" and "God ransom you"
(F¹; K: "God b' wi' you").   *charge* troop, division.   10 *kind kinsman* Westmoreland, whose son had married Salisbury's daughter.   13–14 *And yet . . . of valour*
THEOBALD; F¹ places these lines after line 11, as part of Bedford's speech. The
transposition is followed by all editors.   *mind* remind.   *fram'd* constructed, made.
20–1 *enow . . . loss* enough loss for our country to sustain.

The fewer men, the greater share of honour.
God's will! I pray thee wish not one man more.
By Jove, I am not covetous for gold,
Nor care I who doth feed upon my cost;   25
It yearns me not if men my garments wear;
Such outward things dwell not in my desires:
But if it be a sin to covet honour,
I am the most offending soul alive.
No, faith, my coz, wish not a man from England.   30
God's peace! I would not lose so great an honour
As one man more methinks would share from me
For the best hope I have. O, do not wish one more!
Rather proclaim it, Westmoreland, through my host,
That he which hath no stomach to this fight,   35
Let him depart; his passport shall be made,
And crowns for convoy put into his purse.
We would not die in that man's company
That fears his fellowship to die with us.
This day is call'd the Feast of Crispian.   40
He that outlives this day, and comes safe home,
Will stand a-tiptoe when this day is nam'd
And rouse him at the name of Crispian.
He that shall see this day, and live old age,
Will yearly on the vigil feast his neighbours   45
And say "To-morrow is Saint Crispian."
Then will he strip his sleeve and show his scars,
And say "These wounds I had on Crispin's day."
Old men forget; yet all shall be forgot,
But he'll remember, with advantages,   50

---

23 *God's will* Comparing this interjection with "By Jove" in the next verse, Dr. Johnson remarks that "the king prays like a Christian and swears like a heathen." This is witty, but not sound; for "God's will!" and "God's peace!" (line 31) are oaths, not prayers [K].   25 *upon my cost* at my expense.   26 *yearns me not* does not disturb me.   28 *to covet honour* It has been noted that the King's attitude towards honour is much closer here to that of Hotspur in 1 HENRY IV than to that of the Prince Hal of that play.   30 *coz* cousin (used of any relative outside the immediate family).   35 *stomach to* inclination or taste for.   36 *passport* discharge and guarantee of safe conduct.   37 *convoy* travelling expenses.   39 *fears . . . with us* is afraid to grant me his company by dying with me [K].   40 *Feast of Crispian* October 25 is sacred to two brothers, Crispinus and Crispianus, the

What feats he did that day. Then shall our names,
Familiar in his mouth as household words —
Harry the King, Bedford and Exeter,
Warwick and Talbot, Salisbury and Gloucester —
Be in their flowing cups freshly rememb'red.   55
This story shall the good man teach his son;
And Crispin Crispian shall ne'er go by,
From this day to the ending of the world,
But we in it shall be remembered —
We few, we <u>happy</u> few, we band of brothers;   60
For he to-day that sheds his blood with me
Shall be my brother. Be he ne'er so <u>vile,</u>
This day shall <u>gentle his condition</u>;
And gentlemen in England now abed
Shall think themselves accurs'd they were not here,   65
And hold their manhoods cheap whiles any speaks
That fought with us upon Saint Crispin's day.

Enter Salisbury.

SAL.   My sovereign lord, <u>bestow yourself</u> with speed.
The French are <u>bravely</u> in their <u>battles</u> set
And will with all <u>expedience</u> charge on us.   70

KING.   All things are ready, if our minds be so.

WEST.   Perish the man whose mind is backward now!

KING.   Thou dost not wish more help from England, coz?

WEST.   God's will, my liege! would you and I alone,
Without more help, could fight this royal battle!   75

---

patron saints of shoemakers because, after fleeing from Rome during the reign of
Diocletian, they earned their living as shoemakers until their martyrdom in A.D.
287.   44 *see this day, and live old age* take part in the events of this day and yet
live to be an old man (F¹; POPE, K: "live this day, and see old age").   45 *vigil* eve
of the feast day, celebrated with merriment.   48 *And say . . . Crispin's day* Q¹;
not in F¹.   50 *advantages* additions, exaggeration.   60 *happy* fortunate.   62 *vile*
of lowly birth.   63 *gentle his condition* make him a gentleman.   68 *bestow
yourself* take up your battle station.   69 *bravely* finely, handsomely — referring to
the splendid appearance that they make [K].   *battles* battalions.   70 *expedience*
speed.

KING.　Why, now thou hast <u>unwish'd five thousand men</u>!
　　　　Which <u>likes</u> me better than to wish us one.
　　　　You know your places. God be with you all!

　　　　　　　　Tucket. Enter Montjoy.

MONT.　Once more I come to know of thee, King Harry,
　　　　If for thy ransom thou wilt now <u>compound</u>,　　　80
　　　　Before thy most assured overthrow;
　　　　For certainly thou art so near the <u>gulf</u>
　　　　Thou needs must be <u>englutted</u>. Besides, in mercy,
　　　　The Constable desires thee thou wil<u>t mind</u>
　　　　Thy followers of repentance, that their souls　　85
　　　　May make a peaceful and a sweet retire
　　　　<u>From off</u> these fields, where (wretches!) their poor bodies
　　　　Must lie and fester.

KING.　　　　　　　　Who hath sent thee now?

MONT.　The Constable of France.

KING.　I pray thee bear my former answer back:　　　90
　　　　Bid them <u>achieve</u> me, and then sell my bones.
　　　　Good God! why should they mock poor fellows thus?
　　　　The man that once did sell the lion's skin　⎫
　　　　While the beast liv'd, was kill'd with hunting him⎭
　　　　A many of our bodies shall no doubt　　　　95
　　　　Find <u>native graves</u>; upon the which, I trust,
　　　　Shall <u>witness live in brass</u> of this day's work;
　　　　And those that leave their valiant bones in France,
　　　　Dying like men, though buried in your dunghills,

---

76 *unwish'd five thousand men* The English had about ten thousand men. The King's arithmetic has given the commentators some trouble. Apparently he regards himself and Westmoreland as each representing half of the English forces (as would indeed be the case if the two fought the battle alone), and thinks of Westmoreland as having wished his own half out of existence. But the passage is far from clear [K].　77 *likes* pleases.　80 *compound* settle, make arrangements. 82 *gulf* whirlpool.　83 *englutted* swallowed up.　84 *mind* remind.　87 *From off* F¹; DYCE, K: "From all."　91 *achieve* capture, take possession of.　93-4 *The man . . . hunting him* Shakespeare draws upon Aesop's fable of "The Hunter and the Countryman," substituting a lion for Aesop's bear, possibly because the lion is a more appropriate symbol of royalty.　96 *native graves* graves in their own country — England.　97 *witness live in brass* brass memorial tablets will be erected. These may be commonly seen in Elizabethan churches.　101 *honours reeking* vapours rising like mists. The idea is that the dead men's honours will be drawn up to

They shall be fam'd; for there the sun shall greet them   100
And draw their <u>honours reeking</u> up to heaven,
Leaving their earthly parts to choke your clime,
The smell whereof shall breed a plague in France.
Mark then <u>abounding</u> valour in our English,
That, being dead, like to the bullet's grazing,   105
Break out into a second course of mischief,
Killing <u>in relapse of mortality</u>.
Let me speak proudly. Tell the Constable
We are but warriors <u>for the working</u> day.
Our gayness and our gilt are all besmirch'd   110
With rainy marching in the painful field.
There's not a piece of <u>feather</u> in our host —
Good argument, I hope, we will not fly —
And time hath worn us into <u>slovenry</u>.
But, by the mass, our hearts are <u>in the trim;</u>   115
And my poor soldiers tell me, yet ere night
They'll be in fresher robes, or they will pluck
The gay new coats o'er the French soldiers' heads
And <u>turn them out of service.</u> If they do this
(As, if God please, they shall), my ransom then   120
Will soon be levied. Herald, save thou thy labour.
Come thou no more for ransom, gentle herald.
They shall have none, I swear, but these my joints;
Which if they have <u>as I will leave 'em them,</u>
Shall yield them little, tell the Constable.   125

MONT.   I shall, King Harry. And so fare thee well.

---

heaven by the sun, while their bodies remain to infect the ground on which they died.   104 *abounding* (a) abundant (b) a bounding, rebounding, striking back at those who killed them.   105–7 *That, being dead ... mortality* who will kill while they are dead, just as a bullet which grazes one object harmlessly may kill another on the rebound. *grazing* F²; F¹: "erasing," a variant form. *in relapse of mortality* by a kind of indirect deadliness [ᴋ].   109 *for the working day* i.e. not on a holiday. Fighting is their normal activity.   112 *feather* sign of the gaily dressed gallant.   114 *slovenry* sloppy appearance.   115 *in the trim* (a) handsomely dressed (b) in fine condition.   117–18 *They'll be ... soldiers' heads* they'll have fresher clothing (in some other way) or else they'll pull off the French coats for their own use [ᴋ].   119 *turn them out of service* An Elizabethan servant when dismissed (turned out) had to give up his livery (as the French soldiers will have to give up their coats).   124 *as I will leave 'em them* in the dilapidated condition in which they will be before I fall [ᴋ].

Thou never shalt hear herald any more.   *Exit.*

KING.   I fear thou wilt once more come again <u>for</u> a ransom.

Enter York.

YORK.   My lord, most humbly on my knee I beg
The leading of the <u>vaward</u>.   130

KING.   Take it, brave York. Now, soldiers, march away;
And how thou pleasest, God, dispose the day!   *Exeunt.*

◇◇◇◇◇◇◇◇◇◇◇◇◇◇◇◇◇

[SCENE IV. *The field of battle.*]

Alarum. Excursions. Enter Pistol, French Soldier, Boy.

PIST.   Yield, cur!

FRENCH. Je pense que vous estes le gentilhomme de bonne qualité.

PIST.   Quality! <u>Callino custore me</u>! Art thou a gentleman?
What is thy name? Discuss.

FRENCH. O Signieur Dieu!   5

PIST.   O <u>Signieur Dew</u> should be a gentleman.
Perpend my words, O Signieur Dew, and mark.
O Signieur Dew, thou diest on point of <u>fox</u>,
Except, O Signieur, thou do give to me
Egregious ransom.   10

FRENCH. O, prenez miséricorde! ayez pitié de moi!

PIST.   <u>Moy</u> shall not serve. I will have forty moys;

---

128 *for a* F¹; THEOBALD, K: "for."   130 *vaward* vanguard.
    IV.IV. 3 *Callino custore me* K; F¹: "calmie custore me." Pistol does not under-
stand French, but he catches the word "qualité" and echoes it in a distorted form,
adding some strange words of his own. Malone conjectured that "calmie custure
me" is a misprint for "Calen, o custure me," which Boswell corrected further to
"Callino, castore me." These words appear to be the refrain of an Irish song, and
perhaps we should restore them here. But it is perilous to emend Pistol's gibberish,
and we have no warrant for supposing that he would not murder Irish as badly
as he murders French in this play and Italian in 2 HENRY IV. He probably means
to express contempt and to make an impression on the Frenchman [K].   6 *Signieur
Dew* Pistol takes the Frenchman's terrified exclamation ("Lord God!") as a reply to

                    Or I will fetch thy <u>rim</u> out at thy throat
                    In drops of crimson blood.

FRENCH.   Est-il impossible d'eschapper la force de ton bras?   15

PIST.   <u>Brass,</u> cur?
           Thou damned and <u>luxurious</u> mountain goat,
           Offer'st me brass?

FRENCH.   O, pardonnez-moi!

PIST.   Say'st thou me so? Is that a ton of moys?   20
           Come hither, boy; ask me this slave in French
           What is his name.

BOY.   Escoutez. Comment estes-vous appelé?

FRENCH.   Monsieur le Fer.

BOY.   He says his name is Master Fer.   25

PIST.   Master Fer? <u>I'll fer him,</u> and <u>firk</u> him, and <u>ferret</u> him!
           Discuss the same in French unto him.

BOY.   I do not know the French for "fer," and "ferret," and
           "firk."

PIST.   Bid him prepare, for I will cut his throat.   30

FRENCH.   Que dit-il, monsieur?

BOY.   Il me commande à vous dire que vous faites vous prest;
           car ce soldat ici est disposé tout <u>à cette heure</u> de couper
           vostre gorge.

PIST.   Owy, cuppele gorge, permafoy!   35
           Peasant, unless thou give me crowns, <u>brave</u> crowns;
           Or mangled shalt thou be by this my sword.

his demand for his name. He recognizes "Seigneur" as meaning "Lord," and infers
that his prisoner is a gentleman [K].   8 *fox* sword — so called because those made
of a particularly good kind of steel had the figure of a fox as a trademark on the
blade [K].   12 *Moy* This Pistol takes as a sum of money or a coin. Some suppose he
is thinking of "moidore," a Portuguese gold coin [K].   13 *Or* THEOBALD; F¹: "For."
rim midriff, diaphragm.   16 *Brass* The "s" in "bras" was pronounced in early
seventeenth-century French, so that Pistol's error is not unnatural — for him! [K].
17 *luxurious* lecherous. The goat was a traditional symbol of lechery.   26 *I'll fer
him* Pistol simply repeats the soldier's name with a threatening air [K].   *firk* whip.
ferret worry — as a ferret does a rat [K].   33 *à cette heure* THEOBALD; F¹: "asture," a
common sixteenth-century abbreviated form.   36 *brave* fine.

FRENCH.   O, je vous supplie, pour l'amour de Dieu, me pardonner!
Je <u>suis</u> gentilhomme de bonne maison. Gardez ma vie,
et je vous donnerai deux cents escus.   40

PIST.   What are his words?

BOY.   He prays you to save his life. He is a gentleman of a
good house, and for his ransom he will give you two
hundred crowns.

PIST.   Tell him my fury shall abate, and I   45
The crowns will take.

FRENCH.   Petit monsieur, que dit-il?

BOY.   Encore qu'il est contre son jurement de pardonner
aucun prisonnier, néantmoins, pour les escus que vous
<u>l'avez promis</u>, il est content de vous donner la liberté,   50
le franchisement.

FRENCH.   Sur mes genoux je vous donne mille remercimens; et
je m'estime heureux que <u>je suis tombé</u> entre les mains
d'un chevalier, je pense, le plus brave, vaillant, et très-
distingué seigneur d'Angleterre.   } 55

PIST.   Expound unto me, boy.

BOY.   He gives you, upon his knees, a thousand thanks; and
he esteems himself happy that he hath fall'n into the
hands of one (as he thinks) the most brave, valorous,
and thrice-worthy signieur of England.   60

PIST.   As I suck blood, I will some mercy show!
Follow me, <u>cur</u>.   [*Exit.*]

BOY.   <u>Suivez</u>-vous le grand Capitaine. [*Exit* French Soldier.]
I did never know so full a voice issue from so empty a ⎫
heart; but the saying is true, "The empty vessel makes ⎬ 65
the greatest sound." Bardolph and Nym had ten times ⎭
more valour than this <u>roaring devil</u> i' th' old play that

---

39 *suis* F²; F¹: "suis le."   50 *l'avez promis* MALONE; F¹: "layt a promets."   53 *je suis
tombé* ROWE; F¹: "Ie intombe."   54–5 *très-distingué* CAPELL; F¹: "tres destinie."
62 *cur* Q¹; not in F¹.   63 *Suivez* ROWE; F¹: "saaue."   64–5 *so full . . . a heart* such
bragging speech to issue from so cowardly a person.   67 *roaring devil* The devil
in the moralities was a very boisterous character, but was constantly worried by
the Vice, or clown, who used to offer to pare his long nails with his dagger, which

every one may pare his nails with a wooden dagger; and
they are both hang'd; and so would this be, if he durst
steal anything adventurously. I must stay with the lackeys   70
with the luggage of our camp. The French might have
a good prey of us, if he knew of it; for there is none
to guard it but boys.   *Exit.*

◇◇◇◇◇◇◇◇◇◇◇◇◇◇◇◇◇

[SCENE V. *Another part of the field of battle.*]

Enter Constable, Orleans, Bourbon, Dauphin, *and*
        Rambures.

CON.   O diable!

ORL.   O Seigneur! le jour est perdue, tout est perdu!

DAU.   Mort de ma vie! all is confounded, all!
        Reproach and everlasting shame
        Sits mocking in our plumes.   *A short alarum.*   5
        O méchante fortune! Do not run away.

CON.   Why, all our ranks are broke.

DAU.   O perdurable shame! Let's stab ourselves.
        Be these the wretches that we play'd at dice for?

ORL.   Is this the king we sent to for his ransom?   10

BOUR.   Shame, and eternal shame! nothing but shame!
        Let's die in honour. Once more back again!
        And he that will not follow Bourbon now,
        Let him go hence, and with his cap in hand
        Like a base pander hold the chamber door   15
        Whilst by a slave, no gentler than my dog,
        His fairest daughter is contaminated.

CON.   Disorder, that hath spoil'd us, friend us now!

was palpably made of wood [K].   69 *both hang'd* Thus we learn the fate of Nym
as well as Bardolph.
    IV.v. 3 *Mort de ma vie* ROWE; F¹: "Mort Dieu ma vie." *confounded* ruined, lost.
8 *perdurable* lasting — practically, eternal [K].   12 *honour* Q¹; not in F¹.   16 *by a
slave* Q¹; F¹: "a base slave."   18 *friend* befriend, assist.

Let us <u>on heaps</u> go offer up our lives.

ORL.   We are <u>enow</u> yet living in the field   20
         To smother up the English in our throngs,
         If any order might be thought upon.

BOUR.   The devil take order now! I'll to the throng.
         Let life be short; else shame will be too long.   *Exeunt.*

◇◇◇◇◇◇◇◇◇◇◇◇◇◇◇

[SCENE VI. *Another part of the field.*]

Alarum. Enter the King *and his* Train, [Exeter, *and
    others,] with* Prisoners.

KING.   Well have we done, thrice-valiant countrymen;
         But all's not done, yet keep the French the field.

EXE.   The Duke of York <u>commends him</u> to your Majesty.

KING.   Lives he, good uncle? Thrice within this hour
         I saw him down; thrice up again and fighting.   5
         From helmet to the spur all blood he was.

EXE.   In which array, brave soldier, doth he lie,
         <u>Larding</u> the plain; and by his bloody side,
         Yoke-fellow to his <u>honour-owing</u> wounds,
         The noble Earl of Suffolk also lies.   10
         Suffolk first died; and York, all <u>haggled</u> over,
         Comes to him, where in gore he lay insteep'd,
         And takes him by the beard, kisses the gashes
         That bloodily did <u>yawn</u> upon his face,
         <u>And</u> cries aloud, "Tarry, dear cousin Suffolk!   15
         My soul shall thine keep company to heaven.
         Tarry, sweet soul, for mine, then fly abreast;

---

19 *on heaps* in crowds.   20 *enow* enough.
    IV.VI. 3 *commends him* sends his respects.   8 *Larding* enriching — with his blood
[K].   9 *honour-owing* honour-possessing, honourable.   11 *haggled* hacked and
gashed.   14 *yawn* open wide.   15 *And* Q¹; F¹: "He."   *dear* Q¹; F¹: "my."   21
raught reached.   22 *gripe* grip.   31 *all my mother* all the weakness that I inherited from my mother. Such apologies for weeping were a literary convention in
Elizabethan English [K].   33–4 *I must perforce . . . issue too* I am forced to make
a compromise with my eyes, allowing them to be misty; otherwise they will insist
on weeping outright [K].   *mistful* WARBURTON; F¹: "mixtful."   34 SD *Alarum* call to

As in this glorious and well-foughten field
We kept together in our chivalry!"
Upon these words I came and cheer'd him up.   20
He smil'd me in the face, <u>raught</u> me his hand,
And, with a feeble <u>gripe</u>, says "Dear my lord,
Commend my service to my sovereign."
So did he turn, and over Suffolk's neck
He threw his wounded arm and kiss'd his lips;   25
And so, espous'd to death, with blood he seal'd
A testament of noble-ending love.
The pretty and sweet manner of it forc'd
Those waters from me which I would have stopp'd;
But I had not so much of man in me,   30
And <u>all my mother</u> came into mine eyes
And gave me up to tears.

KING.   I blame you not;
For, hearing this, I must perforce compound
With <u>mistful</u> eyes, or they will issue too.   *Alarum.*
But hark! what new <u>alarum</u> is this same?   35
The French have reinforc'd their scatter'd men.
Then every soldier <u>kill his prisoners!</u>
Give the word through.   *Exeunt.*

◇◇◇◇◇◇◇◇◇◇◇◇◇◇◇◇◇◇

[SCENE VII. *Another part of the field.*]

Enter Fluellen *and* Gower.

FLU.   Kill the poys and the luggage? 'Tis expressly against
the law of arms. 'Tis as arrant a piece of knavery, mark

---

arms. This is the rally which the French nobles talk of in Scene v [K].   37 *kill
his prisoners* A savage, but necessary, order, since the prisoners might revolt, and
the victory be changed to a defeat. Apparently, however, this order was not actually
made effectual till the King learned that the French had massacred the boys and
lackeys left in charge of the camp (see the next scene, lines 9–10) [K]. Shakespeare's
audience might have remembered a similar slaughter of Irish prisoners by Lord
Grey of Wilton at Smerwick in 1579, which was generally regarded in England as
a proper course of action.

you now, as can be offert. In your conscience, now, is it
not?

GOW.   'Tis certain there's <u>not a boy left alive</u>; and the   5
cowardly rascals that ran from the battle ha' done this
slaughter. Besides, they have burned and carried away
all that was in the King's tent; wherefore the King most
worthily hath caus'd every soldier to cut his prisoner's
throat. O, 'tis a gallant king!   10

FLU.   Ay, he was porn <u>at Monmouth</u>, Captain Gower. What
call you the town's name where Alexander the Pig was
born?

GOW.   Alexander the Great.

FLU.   Why, I pray you, is not "pig" great? The pig, or the   15
great, or the mighty, or the huge, or the <u>magnanimous</u>
are all one reckonings, save the phrase is a little
<u>variations.</u>

GOW.   I think Alexander the Great was born in Macedon.
His father was called Philip of Macedon, as I take it.   20

FLU.   I think it is in Macedon where Alexander is porn.
I tell you, Captain, if you look in the maps of the 'orld,
I warrant you sall find, in the comparisons between
Macedon and Monmouth, that the situations, look you,
is both alike. There is a river in Macedon, and there is   25
also moreover a river at Monmouth. It is call'd Wye at
Monmouth; but it is out of my prains what is the name
of the other river. But 'tis all one; 'tis alike as my
fingers is to my fingers, and there is salmons in both. If
you mark Alexander's life well, Harry of Monmouth's   30
life is <u>come after</u> it <u>indifferent well</u>; for there is figures
in all things. Alexander, God knows and you know, in

IV.VII. 5 *not a boy left alive* Falstaff's witty page, then, perished in this massacre.
Thus, of the old retainers of Falstaff, Pistol is the sole survivor [K].   11 *at Monmouth* Fluellen remembers with pride that King Henry was born in Wales [K].   16
magnanimous great of soul, valiant.   18 *variations* He means "various."   31 *is
come after* resembles, follows. *indifferent well* pretty well.   31–2 *there is figures in
all things* Either (a) there is a symbolic likeness in all events of their lives, or (b)
literal agreement must not be expected, for we must allow for figurative language
in making such historical comparisons.   The latter seems better [K].   "Figures" may

his rages, and his furies, and his wraths, and his cholers,
and his moods, and his displeasures, and his indigna-
tions, and also being a little intoxicates in his prains,   35
did, in his ales and his angers, look you, kill his best
friend, <u>Cleitus,</u>

GOW. Our King is not like him in that. He never kill'd any
of his friends.

FLU. It is not well done, mark you now, to take the tales out   40
of my mouth ere it is made and finished. I speak but in
the figures and comparisons of it. As Alexander kill'd
his friend Cleitus, being in his ales and his cups, so also
Harry Monmouth, being in his right wits and his good
judgments, turn'd away the fat knight with the great-   45
belly doublet. He was full of jests, and gipes, and
knaveries, and mocks. I have forgot his name.

GOW. Sir John Falstaff.

FLU. That is he. I'll tell you there is good men porn at
Monmouth.   50

GOW. Here comes his Majesty.

>   *Alarum. Enter* King Harry, [Warwick,
>   Gloucester, Exeter, *and others*,] *with*
>   Prisoners. *Flourish.*

KING. I was not angry since I came to France
       <u>Until this instant</u>. Take a <u>trumpet</u>, herald;
       Ride thou unto the horsemen on yond hill.
       If they will fight with us, bid them come down,   55
       Or <u>void</u> the field. They do offend our sight.
       If they'll do neither, we will come to them
       And make them <u>skirr</u> away as swift as stones

---

mean "comparisons" or "figures of speech."   37 *Cleitus* the friend killed by Alexander at a banquet in Maracanda in 328 B.C., when both were drunk.   45-6 *great-
belly doublet* a kind of doublet (jacket) in which the lower part (called the "belly")
was stuffed with padding (called "bombast") and thus projected out.   53 *Until
this instant* The King's anger is caused by the massacre of the noncombatants and
the pillage of the camp [K].   *trumpet* trumpeter.   56 *void* abandon.   58 *skirr*
scurry.

Enforced from the old Assyrian slings.
Besides, we'll cut the throats of those we have;   60
And not a man of them that we shall <u>take</u>
Shall taste our mercy. Go and tell them so.

Enter Montjoy [*the* Herald].

EXE.   Here comes the herald of the French, my liege.

GLOUC.   His eyes are humbler than they us'd to be.

KING.   How now? What means this, herald? Know'st thou not   65
            That <u>I have fin'd these bones of mine for ransom?</u>
            Com'st thou again for ransom?

HERALD.   No, great King.
            I come to thee for charitable license
            That we may wander o'er this bloody field
            To <u>book</u> our dead, and then to bury them;   70
            To sort our nobles from our common men;
            For many of our princes (woe the while!)
            Lie drown'd and soak'd in <u>mercenary blood</u>;
            So do our <u>vulgar</u> drench their peasant limbs
            In blood of princes<u>; and the</u> wounded steeds   75
            <u>Fret</u> fetlock-deep in gore and with wild rage
            <u>Yerk</u> out their armed heels at their dead masters,
            Killing them twice. O, give us leave, great King,
            To view the field in safety and dispose
            Of their dead bodies!

KING.   I tell thee truly, herald,   80
            I know not if the day be ours or no;
            For yet a many of your horsemen <u>peer</u>
            And gallop o'er the field.

HERALD.   The day is yours.

---

61 *take* capture.   66 *I have fin'd . . . ransom* I have limited my ransom to these
bones of mine — I will give no more. See IV.III,120*off*. The repetition of the word
"ransom" in the next line gives the passage a scornful effect [K].   70 *book* make
a record of (F¹; COLLIER, K: "look").   73 *mercenary blood* the blood of common
soldiers who fight for wages. The great nobles were supposed to render military
service in return for their fiefs, not for money — though in fact, at this time, the
practice had arisen (at least in England) of having contracts entered into between
king and noble by which the latter received a definite sum in return for each

KING.   Praised be God and not our strength for it!
         What is this castle call'd that stands hard by?   85

HERALD. They call it Agincourt.

KING.   Then call we this the field of Agincourt,
         Fought on the day of Crispin Crispianus.

FLU.   Your grandfather of famous memory, an't please your
         Majesty, and your great-uncle Edward the Plack Prince   90
         of Wales, as I have read in the chronicles, fought a
         most prave pattle here in France.

KING.   They did, Fluellen.

FLU.   Your Majesty says very true. If your Majesties is re-
         mem'bred of it, the Welshmen did good service in a   95
         garden where leeks did grow, wearing leeks in their
         Monmouth caps; which your Majesty know to this hour
         is an honourable badge of the service; and I do believe
         your Majesty takes no scorn to wear the leek upon Saint
         Tavy's day.   100

KING.   I wear it for a memorable honour;
         For I am Welsh, you know, good countryman.

FLU.   All the water in Wye cannot wash your Majesty's Welsh
         plood out of your pody, I can tell you that. God pless
         it and preserve it, as long as it pleases his grace, and   105
         his majesty too!

KING.   Thanks, good my countryman.

FLU.   By Jeshu, I am your Majesty's countryman, I care not
         who know it! I will confess it to all the 'orld. I need
         not to be ashamed of your Majesty, praised be God, so   110
         long as your Majesty is an honest man.

---

soldier he furnished. Still the personal service of the noble was not for money [K].
74 *vulgar* commoners.   75 *and the* CAPELL; F¹: "And with."   76 *Fret* chafe.
77 *Yerk* kick.   82 *peer* appear, show themselves.   85 *hard* close.   92 *pattle* the
Battle of Crécy.   97 *Monmouth caps* a kind of cap much worn by the Welsh [K];
they were round and brimless, with a tapering crown.   99 *takes no scorn* is not
ashamed.   99–100 *Saint Tavy's* Saint David's.   101 *memorable honour* honourable
memorial [K].   103–4 *Welsh plood* Henry V's great-grandmother was a Welsh
princess [K].   107 *countryman* Q¹; F¹: "Countrymen."   110 *God* Q¹; F¹: "Good."

KING.   God keep me so!

                    Enter Williams.

                Our heralds go with him.
        Bring me just notice of the numbers dead
        On both our parts.   [*Exeunt* Heralds *with* Montjoy.]
                Call yonder fellow hither.

EXE.   Soldier, you must come to the King.   115

KING.   Soldier, why wear'st thou that glove in thy cap?

WILL.   An't please your Majesty, 'tis the gage of one that I
        should fight withal, if he be alive.

KING.   An Englishman?

WILL.   An't please your Majesty, a rascal that swagger'd with 120
        me last night; who, if 'a live and ever dare to challenge
        this glove, I have sworn to take him a box o' th' ear;
        or if I can see my glove in his cap, which he swore, as
        he was a soldier, he would wear (if alive), I will strike it
        out soundly.   125

KING.   What think you, Captain Fluellen? Is it fit this soldier
        keep his oath?

FLU.   He is a craven and a villain else, an't please your
        Majesty, in my conscience.

KING.   It may be his enemy is a gentleman of great sort, quite 130
        from the answer of his degree.

FLU.   Though he be as good a gentleman as the devil is, as
        Lucifer and Belzebub himself, it is necessary, look your
        Grace, that he keep his vow and his oath. If he be
        perjur'd, see you now, his reputation is as arrant a villain 135
        and a Jacksauce as ever his black shoe trod upon God's
        ground and his earth, in my conscience, la!

---

113 *just* exact.   117 *gage* pledge.   120 *swagger'd* talked braggingly.   121 *'a live*
he lives (CAPELL; F¹: "alive").   122 *take* give.   128 *craven* coward.   129 *conscience*
estimation.   130 *sort* quality, rank.   130–1 *quite from . . . degree* quite exempt
from the necessity of accepting a challenge from a man of Williams's low rank [K].
132 *as good . . . devil is* The devil is a gentleman because his family is the
oldest and most firmly established in hell; he is, of course, the Prince of Darkness.
136 *Jacksauce* saucy fellow. In his excitement Fluellen's English becomes even

KING. Then keep thy vow, sirrah, when thou meet'st the fellow.

WILL. So I will, my liege, as I live.

KING. Who serv'st thou under? 140

WILL. Under Captain Gower, my liege.

FLU. Gower is a good captain and is good knowledge and literatured in the wars.

KING. Call him hither to me, soldier.

WILL. I will, my liege. *Exit.* 145

KING. Here, Fluellen; wear thou this favour for me and stick it in thy cap. When Alençon and myself were down together, I pluck'd this glove from his helm. If any man challenge this, he is a friend to Alençon and an enemy to our person. If thou encounter any such, <u>apprehend</u> 150 him, an thou dost me love.

FLU. Your Grace doo's me as great honours as can be desir'd in the hearts of his subjects. I would fain see the man, that has but two legs, that shall find himself aggrief'd at this glove, that is all. But I would fain see it once, 155 an please God of his grace that I might see.

KING. Know'st thou Gower?

FLU. He is my dear friend, an please you.

KING. Pray thee go seek him and bring him to my tent.

FLU. I will fetch him. *Exit.* 160

KING. My Lord of Warwick, and my brother Gloucester,
Follow Fluellen closely at the heels.
The glove which I have given him for a favour
May <u>haply</u> <u>purchase him</u> a box o' th' ear;
It is the soldier's. I by bargain should 165
Wear it myself. Follow, good cousin Warwick.

---

more uncertain than usual. He uses "Jacksauce," which is good English, in a very inappropriate way [κ]. 147–8 *When Alençon . . . together* The combat between the King and the Duc D'Alençon is described by Holinshed, who reports that the French duke was killed by King Henry's guard when he was about to yield himself a prisoner. 150 *apprehend* arrest. 164 *haply* perhaps. *purchase him* earn for him.

If that the soldier strike him — as I judge
By his blunt bearing, he will keep his word —
Some sudden mischief may arise of it;
For I do know Fluellen valiant,   170
And, <u>touch'd with choler</u>, hot as gunpowder,
And quickly will return an <u>injury</u>.
<u>Follow, and see there be no harm between them</u>.
Go you with me, uncle of Exeter.   *Exeunt.*

❖❖❖❖❖❖❖❖❖❖❖❖❖❖

[SCENE VIII. *Before* King Henry's *pavilion.*]

Enter Gower *and* Williams.

WILL.   <u>I warrant it is to knight you, Captain</u>.

Enter Fluellen.

FLU.   God's will and his pleasure, Captain, I beseech you now,
come <u>apace</u> to the King. There is more good toward you
peradventure than is in your knowledge to dream of.

WILL.   Sir, know you this glove?   5

FLU.   Know the glove? I know the glove is a glove.

WILL.   I know this; and thus I challenge it.   *Strikes him.*

FLU.   <u>'Sblood</u>! an arrant traitor as any's in the universal world,
or in France, or in England!

GOW.   How now, sir? You villain!   10

WILL.   Do you think I'll <u>be forsworn</u>?

FLU.   Stand away, Captain Gower. I will give treason his payment into plows, I warrant you.

---

171 *touch'd with choler* when touched with anger.   172 *injury* insult.   173 *Follow
. . . between them* It is of course impossible for the King to allow Williams to
strike him, for such an act would be high treason. Hence, in order to save Williams's honour, he devises this trick at Fluellen's expense. Of course Fluellen cannot be offended when he knows the truth [K].

IV.VIII. 1 *I warrant . . . Captain* Williams has just delivered the message which
the King has entrusted to him for Captain Gower in IV.VII.144 [K].   3 *apace*

WILL.	I am no traitor.
FLU.	That's a lie in thy throat. I charge you in his Majesty's 15 name <u>apprehend</u> him. He's a friend of the Duke Alençon's.

Enter Warwick *and* Gloucester.

WAR.	How now, how now? What's the matter?
FLU.	My Lord of Warwick, here is (praised be God for it!) a most <u>contagious</u> treason come to light, look you, as you 20 shall <u>desire in a summer's day</u>. Here is his Majesty.

Enter King *and* Exeter.

KING.	How now? What's the matter?
FLU.	My liege, here is a villain and a traitor that, look your Grace, has struck the glove which your Majesty is take out of the helmet of Alençon. 25
WILL.	My liege, this was my glove, here is the fellow of it; and he that I gave it to in <u>change</u> promis'd to wear it in his cap. I promis'd to strike him if he did. I met this man with my glove in his cap, and I have been as good as my word. 30
FLU.	Your Majesty hear now, <u>saving your Majesty's manhood</u>, what an arrant, rascally, beggarly, lousy knave it is! I hope your Majesty is pear me testimony and witness, and will <u>avouchment</u>, that this is the glove of Alençon that your Majesty is give me, in your conscience, now. 35
KING.	Give me thy glove, soldier. Look, here is the fellow of it. 'Twas I indeed thou promised'st to strike; And thou hast given me most <u>bitter terms</u>.
FLU.	An please your Majesty, let his neck answer for it, if there is any martial law in the world. 40

quickly.   8 *'Sblood* by God's blood.   11 *be forsworn* break my oath.   16 *apprehend* arrest.   20 *contagious* Just what word Fluellen here intends is impossible to determine; perhaps he means "outrageous."   21 *desire . . . day* ever wish for. 27 *change* exchange.   31 *saving . . . manhood* An apologetic phrase on account of the abusive words Fluellen intends to use. The meaning is, "In what I say, I have no intention of insulting your honour" [K] — literally, "your manhood being safe."   34 *avouchment* avouch, testify.   38 *bitter terms* harsh words, insults.

KING. How canst thou make me satisfaction?

WILL. All offences, my lord, come from the heart. Never came any from mine that might offend your Majesty.

KING. It was ourself thou didst abuse.

WILL. Your Majesty came not <u>like yourself</u>. You appear'd to 45
me but as a common man; witness the night, your garments, your lowliness. And what your Highness suffer'd
under that shape, I beseech you take it for your own
fault, and not mine; for had you been as I took you for,
I made no offence. Therefore I beseech your Highness 50
pardon me.

KING. Here, uncle Exeter, fill this glove with crowns
And give it to this fellow. Keep it, fellow,
And wear it for an honour in thy cap
Till I do challenge it. Give him the crowns; 55
And, Captain, you must needs be friends with him.

FLU. By this day and this light, the fellow has mettle enough
in his belly. Hold, there is twelve pence for you; and I
pray you to serve God, and keep you out of prawls, and
<u>prabbles,</u> and quarrels, and dissensions, and, I warrant 60
you it is the better for you.

WILL. <u>I will none of your money.</u>

FLU. It is with a good will. I can tell you it will serve you to
mend your shoes. Come, wherefore should you be so
pashful? Your shoes is not so good. 'Tis a good silling, I 65
warrant you, or I will change it.

Enter [*an English*] *Herald.*

KING. Now, herald, are the dead numb'red?

---

45 *like yourself* in your own attire, undisguised.   57–8 *By this day . . . his belly*
As soon as Fluellen knows that it was all the King's joke his resentment is pacified.
It was, of course, an honour for him to act as the King's representative even if the
King was taking liberties with his dignity. The soldier's spirited conduct was of a
kind to approve itself to Fluellen's disposition [K].   60 *prabbles* brabbles, brawls.
62 *I will none of your money* Williams is something of a grumbler and not so

HER.   Here is the number of the slaught'red French.

[*Gives a paper.*]

KING.   What prisoners of <u>good sort</u> are taken, uncle?

EXE.   Charles Duke of Orleans, nephew to the King;   70
John Duke of Bourbon and Lord Bouciqualt:
Of other lords and barons, knights and squires,
Full fifteen hundred, besides common men.

KING.   This <u>note</u> doth tell me of ten thousand French
That in the field lie slain. Of princes, in this number,   75
And nobles bearing <u>banners</u>, there lie dead
One hundred twenty-six; added to these,
Of knights, esquires, and gallant gentlemen,
Eight thousand and four hundred; of the which,
Five hundred were but yesterday dubb'd knights;   80
So that in these ten thousand they have lost
There are but sixteen hundred <u>mercenaries</u>;
The rest are princes, barons, lords, knights, squires,
And gentlemen <u>of blood and quality</u>.
The names of those their nobles that lie dead: 85
Charles Delabreth, High Constable of France;
Jaques of Chatillon, Admiral of France;
The master of the crossbows, Lord Rambures;
Great Master of France, the brave Sir Guichard Dau-
phin;
John Duke of Alençon; Anthony Duke of Brabant,   90
The brother to the Duke of Burgundy;
And Edward Duke of Bar; of lusty earls,
Grandpré and Roussi, <u>Fauconberg</u> and Foix,
Beaumont and Marle, Vaudemont and Lestrale.
Here was a royal fellowship of death!   95
Where is the number of our English dead?

[Herald *gives another paper.*]

---

easily pacified as the more mercurial Fluellen [K].   64–5 *wherefore . . . pashful*
Fluellen takes the soldier's reluctance to be the result of modesty. We must suppose
that in the end Williams takes the shilling, though not with a very good grace [K].
69 *good sort* high rank.   74 *note* list, memorandum.   76 *banners* coats of arms.
82 *mercenaries* common soldiers.   84 *of blood and quality* of noble family and
high rank.   93 *Fauconberg* K: F¹: "Fauconbridge."

<u>Edward the Duke of York</u>, the Earl of Suffolk,
Sir Richard Ketly, Davy Gam, Esquire;
None else of <u>name;</u> and of all other men
<u>But five-and-twenty</u>. O God, thy arm was here!   100
And not to us, but to thy arm alone,
Ascribe we all! When, without stratagem,
But in plain shock and even play of battle,
Was ever known so great and little loss
On one part and on th' other? Take <u>it,</u> God,   105
For it is <u>none but</u> thine!

EXE.   'Tis wonderful!

KING.   Come, go <u>we in procession</u> to the village;
And be it death proclaimed through our host
To boast of this, or take that praise from God
Which is his only.   110

FLU.   Is it not lawful, an please your Majesty, to tell how
many is kill'd?

KING.   Yes, Captain; but with this acknowledgment,
That God fought for us.

FLU.   Yes, my conscience, he did us great good.   115

KING.   Do we all holy rites.
Let there be sung "<u>Non nobis</u>" and "<u>Te Deum</u>,"
The dead <u>with charity</u> enclos'd in clay,
And then to Calais; and to England then;
Where ne'er from France arriv'd more happy men.   120

Exeunt.

---

97 *Edward the Duke of York* He will be remembered as the Aumerle of RICHARD II.
99 *name* rank.   100 *But five-and-twenty* This absurd number is actually handed
down in the chronicles [K]. Actually some 400 or 500 English appear to have been
slain in the battle. The French lost around 10,000 men.   105 *it* i.e. credit for the
victory.   106 *none but* F¹; Q¹, K: "onely."   107 *we in* F²; F¹: "me in."   *procession*
religious procession.   111–12 *Is it not . . . is kill'd* Fluellen, whose Welsh valour
is mingled with an equally Welsh fondness for boasting, is a little distressed at the
thought that the army is to take no credit for itself [K].   117 *"Non nobis" and "Te
Deum"* two well-known psalms.   118 *with charity* with Christian funeral rites.

[Act Five]

◇◇

Enter Chorus.

Vouchsafe to those that have not read the story
That I may prompt them; and of such as have,
I humbly pray them to admit th' excuse
Of time, of numbers, and due course of things
Which cannot in their huge and proper life   5
Be here presented. Now we bear the King
Toward Calais. Grant him there. There seen,
Heave him away upon your winged thoughts
Athwart the sea. Behold, the English beach
Pales in the flood with men, with wives and boys,   10
Whose shouts and claps outvoice the deep-mouth'd sea,
Which, like a mighty whiffler fore the King,
Seems to prepare his way. So let him land,
And solemnly see him set on to London.
So swift a pace hath thought that even now   15
You may imagine him upon Blackheath;
Where that his lords desire him to have borne
His bruised helmet and his bended sword
Before him through the city. He forbids it,
Being free from vainness and self-glorious pride;   20

V. chorus What the Chorus is about to say is necessary information for those in
the audience who have not read the history. For those who have, it may serve as a
reminder of what is omitted on account of the impossibility of presenting all the
details in the theatre [k]. Five years elapsed between the Battle of Agincourt and
the Treaty of Troyes described in this final act. There is no mention of King
Henry's second military expedition to France begun on August 1, 1417.   3–4 *admit
. . . of things* excuse us in our treatment of time etc.   10 *Pales in* encloses as
with a palisade [k].   *men, with wives* F²; F¹: "men, Wiues."   12 *whiffler* a person
who went before the procession to clear the way. Here the sea seems in a similar
manner to announce the coming of King Henry [k].   14 *solemnly* in royal state.
17 *desire* request.

Giving full trophy, signal, and ostent
Quite from himself to God. But now behold,
In the quick forge and working house of thought,
How London doth pour out her citizens!
The Mayor and all his brethren in best sort —   25
Like to the senators of th' antique Rome,
With the plebeians swarming at their heels —
Go forth and fetch their conqu'ring Cæsar in;
As, by a lower but loving likelihood,
Were now the general of our gracious Empress   30
(As in good time he may) from Ireland coming,
Bringing rebellion broached on his sword,
How many would the peaceful city quit
To welcome him! Much more, and much more cause,
Did they this Harry. Now in London place him;   35
As yet the lamentation of the French
Invites the King of England's stay at home;
The Emperor's coming in behalf of France
To order peace between them; and omit
All the occurrences, whatever chanc'd,   40
Till Harry's back-return again to France.
There must we bring him; and myself have play'd
The interim, by rememb'ring you 'tis past.
Then brook abridgment; and your eyes advance,
After your thoughts, straight back again to France.   45

                                                Exit.

21 *signal* trophy, sign of victory. *ostent* show, display. 23 *quick forge . . . of thought* lively and active imaginations. 25 *in best sort* in their finest array and with due ceremony [K]. 28 *fetch* escort. 29 *by a lower but loving likelihood* to use a comparison which is somewhat less in dignity than the thing compared, but which nevertheless we use to show our love. The general referred to in line 30 is Essex, who was now in Ireland attempting to subdue a rebellion. Since Essex was not so high a person as King Henry and the Irish wars were not so important as the French, the comparison is, of course, a lower one, but its employment testifies to the love which the writer has for Essex. As a matter of fact, Essex's return was quite different from that here hoped for [K]. *lower but* SEYMOUR; F¹: "lower, but by." 30 *Empress* A title much affected by Queen Elizabeth. Thus Spenser dedicates his FAERIE QUEENE to her under this designation [K]. 32 *broached* spitted — as if rebellion were a monster which Essex was bringing home on the very sword which had pierced it [K]. 36–7 *the lamentation . . . stay at home* i.e. the French are in such despair that there is no occasion for King Henry to show himself in

◇◇◇◇◇◇◇◇◇◇◇◇◇◇◇◇◇

[SCENE I. *France. The English camp.*]

Enter Fluellen *and* Gower.

GOW. <u>Nay, that's right</u>. But why wear you your leek to-day?
Saint Davy's day is past.

FLU. There is occasions and causes why and wherefore in all
things. I will tell you ass my friend, Captain Gower.
The rascally, <u>scauld</u>, beggarly, lousy, pragging knave,   5
Pistol — which you and yourself and all the world know
to be no petter than a fellow, look you now, of no merits
— he is come to me and prings me pread and salt <u>yester-
day</u>, look you, and bid me eat my leek. It was in a place
where I could not breed no contention with him; but I   10
will be so bold as to wear it in my cap till I see him
once again, and then I will tell him a little piece of my
desires.

Enter Pistol.

GOW. Why, here he comes, swelling like a turkey cock.

FLU. 'Tis no matter for his swellings nor his turkey cocks.   15
God pless you, Aunchient Pistol! you scurvy, lousy knave,
God pless you!

_____

France at present [K].   38 *The Emperor* The Holy Roman Emperor, Sigismund,
who came to England in May, 1416, to intercede on behalf of France.   39 *order*
arrange the terms of.   42 *There must we bring him* This prepares the audience for
the place of the next scenes, namely, France, and gives them to understand that
in the meantime the King has returned to England and gone back to France
again [K].   42-3 *have . . . interim* have taken the place of the actors who would
have represented what has gone on in the interval between Act IV and Act V [K].
43 *rememb'ring* reminding.   44 *brook abridgment* put up with or be indulgent
to our cutting down the full history [K].

V.I. 1 *Nay, that's right* As so often is the case, we hear only the end of the conversation. These words refer to something which Fluellen has said; we have no
means of knowing what [K].   5 *scauld* scurvy.   8-9 *yesterday* i.e. on St. David's
Day, when the leek was worn, as was customary on that day. St. David is the patron
saint of the Welsh. Nobody knows how the custom originated [K].

PIST.   Ha! art thou bedlam? Dost thou thirst, base Troyan,
To have me fold up Parca's fatal web?
Hence! I am qualmish at the smell of leek.   20

FLU.   I peseech you heartily, scurvy, lousy knave, at my desires,
and my requests, and my petitions, to eat, look you, this
leek. Because, look you, you do not love it, nor your affections and your appetites and your disgestions doo's
not agree with it, I would desire you to eat it.   25

PIST.   Not for Cadwallader and all his goats.

FLU.   There is one goat for you. (*Strikes him.*) Will you be so
good, scauld knave, as eat it?

PIST.   Base Troyan, thou shalt die!

FLU.   You say very true, scauld knave, when God's will is. I   30
will desire you to live in the meantime, and eat your
victuals. Come, there is sauce for it. [*Strikes him.*] You
call'd me yesterday mountain-squire; but I will make you
to-day a squire of low degree. I pray you fall to. If you
can mock a leek, you can eat a leek.   35

GOW.   Enough, Captain. You have astonish'd him.

FLU.   I say I will make him eat some part of my leek, or I will
peat his pate four days. — Bite, I pray you. It is good for
your green wound and your ploody coxcomb.

PIST.   Must I bite?   40

FLU.   Yes, certainly, and out of doubt, and out of question too,
and ambiguities.

PIST.   By this leek, I will most horribly revenge! I eat, and yet,
I swear —

---

18 *bedlam* a lunatic. *Troyan* Trojan — a slang term for a rascal. 19 *fold . . . web*
i.e. put an end to their life. The Parcæ were the Roman Fates. Pistol thinks of
them here as weaving the web of a man's life. To "fold up" this web would then
be "to abbreviate the life" [K]. 23–4 *affections* feelings. 24 *disgestions* digestions
— not a blunder of Fluellen's, for the form was common [K]. 26 *Cadwallader*
Cadwallader the Great, the last of the Welsh kings, whom Pistol here takes pleasure in representing as a goatherd merely. Of course, this is an insult to all Welshmen [K]. 33 *mountain-squire* a poverty-stricken squire from the barren mountains
of Wales [K]. 34 *squire of low degree* An allusion to a very popular metrical
romance, composed in the fifteenth century and well-known in Shakespeare's time.

FLU.	Eat, I pray you. Will you have some more sauce to your 45 leek? There is not enough leek to swear by.
PIST.	Quiet thy cudgel. Thou dost see I eat.
FLU.	Much good do you, scauld knave, heartily. Nay, pray you throw none away. The skin is good for your <u>broken</u> coxcomb. When you take occasions to see leeks hereafter, 50 I pray you mock at 'em; that is all.
PIST.	<u>Good</u>.
FLU.	Ay, leeks is good. Hold you, there is a groat to heal your pate.
PIST.	Me a groat? 55
FLU.	Yes, verily and in truth, you shall take it; or I have an- other leek in my pocket, which you shall eat.
PIST.	<u>I take thy groat in earnest of revenge.</u>
FLU.	If I owe you anything, I will pay you in cudgels. You shall be a woodmonger and buy nothing of me but cudg- 60 els. <u>God buy you</u>, and keep you, and heal your pate.
	Exit.
PIST.	All hell shall stir for this!
GOW.	Go, go. You are a counterfeit cowardly knave. Will you mock at an ancient tradition, <u>begun</u> upon an honourable respect and worn as a memorable trophy of predeceased 65 valour, and dare not avouch in your deeds any of your words? I have seen you <u>gleeking</u> and <u>galling</u> at this gen- tleman twice or thrice. You thought, because he could

Of course Fluellen means that he will humble Pistol [K]. 36 *astonish'd* stunned,
overcome (much stronger than in modern usage). 39 *green* raw. *coxcomb* head.
43 *and yet* GRANT WHITE; F¹: "and eat." 49 *broken* bleeding. 52 *Good* Pistol says
this with all the awful significance of a threat, but Fluellen chooses to take it as
if he had commended the leek which he is eating [K]. 58 *I take . . . revenge*
"Earnest" is properly a small sum of money paid on the conclusion of a bargain
to bind the transaction. Here, of course, Pistol means that he takes this money to
remind him that he owes Fluellen revenge [K]. 61 *God buy you* F¹; K: "God b' wi'
you." 64 *begun* CAPELL; F¹: "began." 64-5 *upon an honourable respect* for an
honourable reason. 67 *gleeking* mocking. *galling* irritating, making satirical re-

not speak English in the native garb, he could not there-
fore handle an English cudgel. You find it otherwise; and 70
henceforth let a Welsh correction teach you a good Eng-
lish condition. Fare ye well. *Exit.*

PIST. Doth Fortune play the huswife with me now?
News have I, that my Nell is dead i' th' spital
Of malady of France; 75
And there my rendezvous is quite cut off.
Old I do wax, and from my weary limbs
Honour is cudgell'd. Well, bawd will I turn,
And something lean to cutpurse of quick hand.
To England will I steal, and there I'll steal; 80
And patches will I get unto these cudgell'd scars
And swear I got them in the Gallia wars. *Exit.*

◇◇◇◇◇◇◇◇◇◇◇◇◇◇◇◇◇

[SCENE II.
France. The French King's *Palace.*]

Enter, at one door, King Henry, Exeter, Bedford,
[Gloucester,] Warwick, [Westmoreland,] *and other*
Lords; *at another,* Queen Isabel, *the* [French] King,
the Duke of Burgundy, [*the* Princess Katherine,
Alice,] *and other* French.

KING H. Peace to this meeting, wherefore we are met!
Unto our brother France and to our sister
Health and fair time of day. Joy and good wishes

---

marks. 69 *garb* fashion. 71–2 *a good . . . condition* proper behaviour for an
Englishman. 73 *play the huswife* play the hussy, betray me. Fortune is constantly
spoken of as an unfaithful mistress because she smiles upon all men but is constant
to none [K]. 74 *my Nell* CAPELL; F¹: "my Doll." *spital* hospital. 75 *Of* POPE; F¹:
"Of a." *malady of France* venereal disease. 77–8 *from my . . . cudgell'd* Having
been publicly cudgelled without instantly killing his assailant, Pistol's honour as a
gentleman and a soldier was of course quite gone [K]. 78 *bawd* pander. 79
something lean . . . hand i.e. show a certain inclination to the profession of
Nimblefinger Cutpurse. This profession, as well as that of pandering, had been
cultivated by Pistol before he went to the wars [K]. 82 *swear* F³; F¹: "swore."

V.II. 1 *Peace . . . are met* peace be to this assembly, and it is precisely for
that purpose (namely, to make peace) that we have come together [K]. 5 *royalty*
royal family. 6 *contriv'd* arranged, organized. 12 *England* F²; F¹: "Ireland."

To our most fair and princely cousin Katherine.
And as a branch and member of this royalty,   5
By whom this great assembly is contriv'd,
We do salute you, Duke of Burgundy.
And, princes French, and peers, health to you all!

FRANCE. Right joyous are we to behold your face,
Most worthy brother England. Fairly met.   10
So are you, princes English, every one.

QUEEN. So happy be the issue, brother England,
Of this good day and of this gracious meeting
As we are now glad to behold your eyes —
Your eyes which hitherto have borne in them,   15
Against the French that met them in their bent,
The fatal balls of murdering basilisks.
The venom of such looks, we fairly hope,
Have lost their quality, and that this day
Shall change all griefs and quarrels into love.   20

KING H. To cry amen to that, thus we appear.

QUEEN. You English princes all, I do salute you.

BURG. My duty to you both, on equal love,
Great Kings of France and England! That I have la-
bour'd
With all my wits, my pains, and strong endeavours   25
To bring your most imperial Majesties
Unto this bar and royal interview,
Your mightiness on both parts best can witness.
Since, then, my office hath so far prevail'd

---

16 *in their bent* as they were directed, in their glance.   17 *The fatal . . . basilisks*
This line involves an elaborate double meaning. (a) The basilisk was a fabulous
monster of the serpent kind, which was supposed to kill by the venomous emana-
tions from its eyeballs, so that its glance meant death. (b) The name "basilisk" was
also given to a certain kind of cannon, so called because originally it bore the
figure of a basilisk [K]. "Balls" is thus used as (a) eyeballs (b) cannon balls.   19
quality nature, essential quality.   20 *griefs* grievances.   23 *on equal love* in consequence of the equal love that I bear to you both [K].   27 *Unto this bar* There was
a bar fixed between the French dignitaries and the English when the interview actually took place, and we must suppose that this was also represented on the stage
[K]. A wooden bar was a conventional device to indicate court scenes on the Elizabethan stage.   29 *my office* my good offices, my services [K].

That, face to face and royal eye to eye,   30
You have <u>congreeted</u>, let it not disgrace me
If I demand, <u>before this royal view</u>,
What <u>rub</u> or what impediment there is
Why that the naked, poor, and mangled Peace,
Dear nurse of arts, <u>plenty</u>, and joyful births,   35
Should not, in this best garden of the world,
Our fertile France, <u>put up her lovely visage</u>.
Alas, she hath from France too long been chas'd!
And <u>all her husbandry doth lie on heaps</u>,
Corrupting in <u>it</u> own fertility.   40
Her vine, the merry cheerer of the heart,
Unpruned dies; her hedges <u>even-pleach'd</u>,
Like prisoners wildly overgrown with hair,
Put forth disorder'd twigs; her fallow <u>leas</u>
<u>The darnel, hemlock, and rank fumitory</u>   45
Doth root upon, while that the <u>coulter</u> rusts
That should <u>deracinate such savagery</u>.
The even mead, that <u>erst</u> brought sweetly forth
The freckled cowslip, <u>burnet</u>, and green clover,
Wanting the scythe, <u>all</u> <u>uncorrected</u>, <u>rank</u>,   50
<u>Conceives by idleness</u> and <u>nothing teems</u>
But hateful docks, rough thistles, kecksies, burrs,
Losing both beauty and utility.
And <u>as our</u> vineyards, fallows, meads, and hedges,
<u>Defective in their natures</u>, grow to wildness,   55
Even so our <u>houses</u> and ourselves and children
Have lost, or do not learn for want of time,

---

31 *congreeted* exchanged greetings, met together.   32 *before this royal view* in the presence of these kings.   33 *rub* impediment (a term from the game of bowls).   35 *plenty* DYCE; F¹: "Plentyes."   37 *put up her lovely visage* i.e. raise it from the ground where she lies prostrate; or, perhaps, simply show her face, since the idea seems to be that she has been driven out of France [K].   39 *all her . . . heaps* the extent of her agriculture is the accumulation of refuse heaps.   40 *it* its (an old genitive form).   42 *even-pleach'd* even-plaited — with the ends twined so as to present an even surface, as was often done with hedges [K].   44 *leas* meadows, open fields.   45 *The darnel . . . fumitory* three types of weed which grow most prolifically on land which has been ploughed. *fumitory* F⁴; F¹: "Femetary."   46 *coulter* plough blade.   47 *deracinate such savagery* root up such wild growth.   48 *erst* formerly.   49 *burnet* a kind of fodder [K].   50 *all* ROWE; F¹: "withall." *uncorrected* undisciplined. *rank* overgrown.   51 *Conceives by idleness* that is to say,

  The sciences that should become our country;
  But grow like savages — as soldiers will,
  That nothing do but meditate on blood —   60
  To swearing and stern looks, <u>diffus'd</u> attire,
  And everything that seems unnatural.
  Which to <u>reduce</u> into our former <u>favour</u>
  You are assembled; and my speech entreats
  That I may know the <u>let</u> why gentle Peace   65
  Should not expel these <u>inconveniences</u>
  And bless us with her former qualities.

KING H. If, Duke of Burgundy, you <u>would</u> the peace
  Whose want gives growth to th' imperfections
  Which you have cited, you must buy that peace   70
  With full accord to all our just demands;
  Whose <u>tenures</u> and <u>particular effects</u>
  You have, <u>enschedul'd</u> briefly, in your hands.

BURG. The King hath heard them; to the which as yet
  There is no answer made.

KING H.   Well then, the peace,   75
  Which you before so <u>urg'd</u>, lies in his answer.

FRANCE. I have but with a <u>cursitory</u> eye
  O'erglanc'd the articles. Pleaseth your Grace
  To appoint some of your Council <u>presently</u>
  To sit with us once more, with better heed   80
  To resurvey them, we will <u>suddenly</u>
  <u>Pass our accept and peremptory</u> answer.

KING H. Brother, we shall. Go, uncle Exeter,

---

is fertilized with useless weeds [K]. *nothing teems* brings forth nothing.   52
kecksies A kex is a dry hemlock shoot or the like [K].   54 *as our* CAPELL; F¹: "all
our."   55 *Defective in their natures* losing their true natures, which is to bring
forth useful plants, and the like [K].   56 *houses* households.   61 *diffus'd* dis-
ordered.   63 *reduce* lead back, return. *favour* good appearance.   65 *let* hindrance,
obstacle.   66 *inconveniences* improper or unbecoming things [K].   68 *would*
would like to have, desire.   72 *tenures* tenours, general demands. *particular ef-
fects* special provisions.   73 *enschedul'd* drawn up in the form of a schedule [K].
76 *urg'd* argued in support of.   77 *cursitory* cursory (WILSON; F¹: "curselarie"; Q³,
K: "cursorary").   79 *presently* at once.   81 *suddenly* immediately — containing the
notion of rapidity without that of abruptness [K].   82 *Pass . . . answer* settle
upon what we can accept and give an answer which shall be final so far as we are
concerned [K]. *peremptory* final.

And brother Clarence, and you, brother Gloucester,
Warwick, and Huntingdon — go with the King;   85
And take with you free power to ratify,
Augment, or alter, as your wisdoms best
Shall see advantageable for our dignity,
Anything <u>in or out of our demands</u>;
And we'll <u>consign</u> thereto. Will you, fair sister,   90
Go with the princes or stay here with us?

QUEEN.   Our gracious brother, I will go with them.
<u>Happily</u> a woman's voice may do some good
<u>When articles too nicely urg'd be stood on</u>.

KING H.   Yet leave our cousin Katherine here with us.   95
She is our <u>capital</u> demand, compris'd
Within the fore-rank of our articles.

QUEEN.   She hath good leave.

                              Exeunt. Manent King Henry, Kath-
                              erine, *and the* Gentlewoman [Alice].

KING H.   Fair Katherine, and most fair!
Will you vouchsafe to teach a soldier terms
Such as will enter at a lady's ear   100
And plead his love suit to her gentle heart?

KATH.   Your Majesty shall mock at me. I cannot speak your
England.

KING H.   O fair Katherine, if you will love me soundly with your
French heart, I will be glad to hear you confess it 105
brokenly with your English tongue. Do you like me,
Kate?

KATH.   Pardonnez-moi, I cannot tell <u>wat</u> is "like me."

---

89 *in or out of our demands* whether included in our demands or not.   90 *con-sign* agree formally. To "consign" literally means "to seal together with" and so "to consent in a most solemn way" [K].   93 *Happily* perhaps.   94 *When articles . . . stood on* when things or demands, the mention of which is too punctilious or particular, are insisted on or made a point of [K].   96 *capital* chief, most important.   108 *wat* F¹; ROWE, K: "vat."   110 *Que dit-il . . . anges* Katherine's readiness in understanding a compliment in English is a pretty touch [K].   120 *The Princess . . . Englishwoman* i.e. she has a true English modesty and common sense in the matter of trusting compliments [K].   123 *such a plain king* As a matter of fact, the King was highly accomplished. He was anything but a farmer-like person. We have our choice, then, in the present case between two suppositions. Either Shakespeare (a) was describing a different kind of man from Prince Hal or

KING H.   An angel is like you, Kate, and you are like an angel.

KATH.   Que dit-il? Que je suis semblable à les anges?   110

ALICE.   Oui, vraiment, sauf vostre grâce, ainsi dit-il.

KING H.   I said so, dear Katherine, and I must not blush to affirm
          it.

KATH.   O bon Dieu! les langues des hommes sont pleines de
          tromperies.   115

KING H.   What says she, fair one? that the tongues of men are full
          of deceits?

ALICE.   Oui, dat de tongues of de mans is be full of deceits. Dat
          is de Princesse.

KING H.   The Princess is the better Englishwoman. I' faith, Kate, 120
          my wooing is fit for thy understanding. I am glad thou
          canst speak no better English; for if thou couldst, thou
          wouldst find me such a plain king that thou wouldst
          think I had sold my farm to buy my crown. I know no
          ways to mince it in love but directly to say "I love you." 125
          Then, if you urge me farther than to say, "Do you in
          faith?" I wear out my suit. Give me your answer; i' faith,
          do! and so clap hands and a bargain. How say you, lady?

KATH.   Sauf vostre honneur, me understand well.

KING H.   Marry, if you would put me to verses or to dance for 130
          your sake, Kate, why, you undid me. For the one I have
          neither words nor measure; and for the other I have no
          strength in measure, yet a reasonable measure in
          strength. If I could win a lady at leapfrog, or by vault-
          ing into my saddle with my armour on my back, under 135
          the correction of bragging be it spoken, I should quickly

---

(b) the King is representing himself as far plainer than he actually is [K]. Shakespeare is probably concerned with stressing the conventional Renaissance antithesis
between the soldier and the lover, the one a straightforward, plain-spoken man of
action, and the other one who must master the elaborate language of compliment
by which ladies must be wooed. The King's scholarly accomplishments, of which
we have been amply informed in the first act, are not at issue here.   125 *to mince
it* to mince matters, to speak delicately, like a courtier [K].   127 *wear out my suit*
have used up my resources as a wooer [K].   128 *clap hands* clasp hands to seal the
bargain.   131 *undid me* would ruin me.   132 *nor measure* nor metre.   133 *in
measure* A measure was a kind of stately court dance [K].   *measure in* quantity of.
135-6 *under . . . bragging* without being censured for bragging.

leap into a wife. Or if I might <u>buffet</u> for my love, or
<u>bound my horse</u> for her favors, I could lay on like a
butcher and sit like a <u>jackanapes</u>, never off. But, before
God, Kate, I cannot <u>look greenly</u> nor gasp out my elo-   140
quence, nor I have no <u>cunning</u> in protestation; only
downright oaths, which I never use till urg'd, nor never
break for urging. If thou canst love a fellow of this
temper, Kate, <u>whose face is not worth sun-burning</u>, that
never looks in his glass for love of anything he sees there,   145
<u>let thine eye be thy cook.</u> I speak to thee <u>plain soldier</u>.
If thou canst love me for this, take me; if not, to say to
thee that I shall die, is true — but for thy love, by the
Lord, no; yet I love thee too. And while thou liv'st, dear
Kate, take a fellow of plain and <u>uncoined</u> constancy; for   150
he perforce must do thee right, because he hath not the
gift to woo in other places. For these fellows of infinite
tongue that can rhyme themselves into ladies' favours,
they do always reason themselves out again. What! A
speaker is but a <u>prater</u>; a rhyme is but a ballad. A good   155
leg <u>will fall</u>, a straight back will stoop, a black beard
will turn white, a curl'd pate will grow bald, a fair face
will wither, a full eye will wax hollow; but a good heart,
Kate, is the sun and the moon; or rather, the sun, and
not the moon, for it shines bright and never changes, but   160
keeps his course truly. If thou would have such a one,
take me; and take me, take a soldier; take a soldier, take
a king. And what say'st thou then to my love? Speak, my
fair — and fairly, I pray thee.

KATH.   Is it possible dat I sould love de ennemie of France?   165

KING H.   No, it is not possible you <u>should love</u> the enemy of
France, Kate; but in loving me you should love the

---

137 *buffet* box.   138 *bound my horse* make my horse jump.   139 *jackanapes* ape.
The reference is to performing apes that ride horseback [k].   140 *look greenly*
look foolish. The King's contemptuous phrase for the moonstruck, sentimental
looks of lovers [k].   141 *cunning* skill.   144 *whose face . . . sun-burning* whose
complexion is so rugged that the sun takes no pleasure in spoiling it [k].   146 *let
thine eye be thy cook* i.e. let your eye dress my face and make it attractive, as the
cook by his artistry makes the simple matter of nature appear attractive. The expression may have been proverbial.   *plain soldier* in plain soldier's talk.   150

friend of France; for I love France so well that I will not
part with a village of it — I will have it all mine. And,
Kate, when France is mine and I am yours, then yours is 170
France and you are mine.

KATH.   I cannot tell wat is dat.

KING H.   No, Kate? I will tell thee in French; which I am sure
will hang upon my tongue like a new-married wife about
her husband's neck, hardly to be shook off. Quand j'ai 175
la possession de France, et quand vous avez la possession
de moi (Let me see, what then? Saint Denis be my
speed!), donc vostre est France et vous estes mienne. It
is as easy for me, Kate, to conquer the kingdom as to
speak so much more French. I shall never move thee in 180
French, unless it be to laugh at me.

KATH.   Sauf vostre honneur, le François que vous parlez, il est
meilleur que l'Anglois lequel je parle.

KING H.   No, faith, is't not, Kate. But thy speaking of my tongue,
and I thine, most truly-falsely, must needs be granted 185
to be much at one. But, Kate, dost thou understand thus
much English? Canst thou love me?

KATH.   I cannot tell.

KING H.   Can any of your neighbours tell, Kate? I'll ask them.
Come, I know thou lovest me; and at night when you 190
come into your closet, you'll question this gentlewoman
about me; and I know, Kate, you will to her dispraise
those parts in me that you love with your heart; but,
good Kate, mock me mercifully; the rather, gentle Princess, because I love thee cruelly. If ever thou beest mine, 195

---

uncoined sincere, uncounterfeited. A "coiner" was a false coiner or counterfeiter [K].
155 *prater* one who talks foolishly.   156 *will fall* will shrink, grow old and
withered.   166 *should love* would certainly love.   172 *wat* F¹; ROWE, K: "vat."
175 *Quand j'ai* POPE; F¹: "Ie quand sur." If Shakespeare intended to indicate the
utter hopelessness of Henry's French, the emendation may be unwarranted.   177
Saint Denis The King swears appropriately enough by the national saint of France
[K].   177-8 *be my speed* help me to success.   182 *que* K; F¹: "ques."   182-3 *est
meilleur* K; F¹: "melius."   186 *at one* alike.   191 *closet* private room.

Kate — as I have _a saving faith_ within me tells me thou
shalt — I get thee _with scambling,_ and thou must therefore needs prove a good soldier-breeder. Shall not thou
and I, between Saint Denis and Saint George, compound
a boy, half French, half English, that shall go to Con-⎫200
stantinople and take the Turk by the beard?/Shall we⎭
not? What say'st thou, my fair _flower-de-luce_?

KATH.   I do not know dat.

KING H.   No; 'tis hereafter to know, but now to promise. Do but
now promise, Kate, you will endeavour for your French 205
part of such a boy; and for my English moiety take the
word of a king and a _bachelor._ How answer you, la plus
belle Katherine du monde, mon très-cher et devin déesse?

KATH.   Your Majestee ave fausse French enough to deceive de
most sage damoisell dat is en France.   210

KING H.   Now, fie upon my false French! By mine honour in true
English, I love thee, Kate; by which honour I dare not
swear thou lovest me; yet my _blood_ begins to flatter me
that thou dost, notwithstanding the poor and _untemper-_
ing effect of my visage. Now _beshrew_ my father's ambi- 215
tion! He was thinking of civil wars when he _got_ me;
therefore was I created with a _stubborn_ outside, with an
aspect of iron, that, when I come to woo ladies, I fright
them. But in faith, Kate, the elder I wax, the better I
shall appear. My comfort is, that old age, that _ill layer-up_ 220
of beauty, can do no more spoil upon my face. Thou
hast me, if thou hast me, at the worst; and thou shalt
wear me, if thou wear me, better and better; and therefore tell me, most fair Katherine, will you have me?
Put off your maiden blushes; _avouch_ the thoughts of 225
your heart with the looks of an empress; take me by the

196 _a saving faith_ a faith which leads to salvation. A common religious expression. Its use by the King shows how unsafe it is to infer that all such phrases were
regarded by Shakespeare as Puritanical [K].   197 _with scambling_ by warfare (literally, "scrambling") [K].   200–201 _a boy . . . the beard_ It is ironic that this boy,
King Henry VI, should be incapable, not only of leading a crusade, but even of
maintaining his father's conquests in France and keeping his own crown.   202
flower-de-luce fleur-de-lis, the national emblem of France.   207 _bachelor_ young
fellow, young knight [K].   213 _blood_ inclination, natural impulse.   214–15 _un-_

hand, and say "Harry of England, I am thine!" which
word thou shalt no sooner bless mine ear <u>withal</u> but I
will tell thee aloud "England is thine, Ireland is thine,
France is thine, and Henry Plantagenet is thine"; who, 230
though I speak it before his face, if he be not fellow
with the best king, thou shalt find the best king of good
fellows. Come, your answer in <u>broken music</u>! for thy
voice is music and thy English broken; therefore, queen
<u>of all, Katherine, break</u> thy mind to me in broken Eng- 235
lish. Wilt thou have me?

KATH.　Dat is as it sall please de roi mon père.

KING H.　Nay, it will please him well, Kate. It shall please him,
Kate.

KATH.　Den it sall also content me. 240

KING H.　Upon that I kiss your hand and I call you my queen.

KATH.　Laissez, mon seigneur, laissez, laissez! Ma foi, je ne veux
point que vous abaissiez vostre grandeur en baisant la
main d'une de vostre Seigneurie indigne serviteur. Excusez-moi, je vous supplie, mon très-puissant seigneur. 245

KING H.　Then I will kiss your lips, Kate.

KATH.　Les dames et demoiselles pour estre baisées devant leur
noces, il n'est pas la coutume de France.

KING H.　Madam my interpreter, what says she?

ALICE.　Dat it is not be de fashon pour de ladies of France — I 250
cannot tell <u>wat</u> is "<u>baiser</u>" en Anglish.

KING H.　To kiss.

ALICE.　Your Majestee entendre bettre que moi.

KING H.　It is not a fashion for the maids in France to kiss before
they are married, would she say? 255

---

tempering unattractive. To "temper" often means to "influence," to "work to
one's will." The King means that his face is not "winning" [K].　215 *beshrew*
confound, curse.　216 *got* begot.　217 *stubborn* rude, rough.　220 *ill layer-up*
poor preserver — i.e. wrinkler.　225 *avouch* declare.　228 *withal* with.　233 *broken
music* music arranged to be played in parts by different instruments.　235 *of all,
Katherine* F¹; CAPELL, K: "of all Katherines." *break* broach, utter.　251 *wat* F¹;
ROWE, K: "vat." *baiser* HANMER; F¹: "buisse."

ALICE. Oui, vraiment.

KING H. O Kate, <u>nice</u> customs <u>curtsy</u> to great kings. Dear Kate,
you and I cannot be confin'd within the weak <u>list</u> of a
country's fashion. We are the makers of manners, Kate;
and the liberty <u>that follows our places</u> stops the mouth 260
of all find-faults, as I will do yours for upholding the
nice fashion of your country in denying me a kiss. Therefore patiently, and yielding. [*Kisses her.*] You have witch-
craft in your lips, Kate. There is more eloquence in a
sugar touch of them than in the tongues of the French 265
Council, and they should sooner persuade Harry of England than a general petition of monarchs. Here comes
your father.

> *Enter the* French Power *and the* Eng-
> lish Lords.

BURG. God save your Majesty! My royal cousin,
Teach you our princess English? 270

KING H. I would have her learn, my fair cousin, how perfectly I
love her, and that is good English.

BURG. Is she not apt?

KING H. Our tongue is rough, coz, and my <u>condition</u> is not
smooth; so that, having neither the voice nor the heart 275
of flattery about me, I cannot so conjure up the spirit of
love in her that he will appear in his true likeness.

BURG. Pardon the frankness of my mirth if I answer you for
that. If you would conjure in her, you must make a circle; if conjure up love in her in his true likeness, he must 280
appear <u>naked and blind</u>. Can you blame her then, being
a maid yet ros'd over with the virgin crimson of modesty,
if she deny the appearance of a naked blind boy in her

---

257 *nice* precise, punctilious.   *curtsy* bow (f¹, k: "cursy." an Elizabethan variant).   258 *list* barrier, limitations.   260 *that follows our places* that is permitted
to those in our positions.   274 *condition* disposition, character.   281 *naked and
blind* as Cupid was conventionally depicted.   285 *consign* agree.   286 *wink* shut
their eyes.   292 *summer'd* nurtured (as animals are fed during the summer
months).   293 *Bartholomeu-tide* August 24, when flies grow sluggish as Autumn
approaches.   296 *moral* symbol — that of the late summer fly.   301-2 *who cannot*

| | naked seeing self? It were, my lord, a hard condition for a maid to _consign_ to. | 285 |

KING H.   Yet they do _wink_ and yield, as love is blind and enforces.

BURG.   They are then excus'd, my lord, when they see not what they do.

KING H.   Then, good my lord, teach your cousin to consent wink-
           ing.   290

BURG.   I will wink on her to consent, my lord, if you will teach
           her to know my meaning; for maids well _summer'd_ and
           warm kept are like flies at _Bartholomew-tide_, blind,
           though they have their eyes; and then they will endure
           handling which before would not abide looking on.   295

KING H.   This _moral_ ties me over to time and a hot summer; and
           so I shall catch the fly, your cousin, in the latter end,
           and she must be blind too.

BURG.   As love is, my lord, before it loves.

KING H.   It is so; and you may, some of you, thank love for my   300
           blindness, who cannot see many a fair French city for
           one fair French maid that stands in my way.

FRANCE.   Yes, my lord, you see them _perspectively_ — the cities
           turn'd into a maid; for they are all girdled with maiden
           walls that war hath _never_ ent'red.   305

KING H.   Shall Kate be my wife?

FRANCE.   So please you.

KING H.   I am content, so the maiden cities you talk of may wait
           on her. So the maid that stood in the way for my wish
           shall show me the way to my will.   310

FRANCE.   We have consented to all _terms of reason_.

KING H.   Is't so, my lords of England?

WEST.   The King hath granted every article:

... _my way_ He means that, out of his love for Katherine, he is willing to give up
many French cities which he might possess [K].   303 _perspectively_ as through a
perspective glass — a kind of optical toy which distorts objects. It was in great
favour with the Elizabethans and is often mentioned [K].   305 _never_ ROWE; not in
F¹.   308–9 _wait on her_ go along with her (as part of her dowry).   311 _terms of
reason_ reasonable terms.

His daughter first; and in sequel, all,
<u>According to their firm proposed natures.</u>　315

EXE.　Only he hath not yet subscribed this: <u>Where</u> your Majesty demands that the King of France, having any occasion to write <u>for matter of grant</u>, shall name your Highness in this form and with this <u>addition</u>, in French, "Nostre très-cher fils Henri, Roi d'Angleterre, héritier de 320 France"; and thus in Latin, "<u>Praeclarissimus</u> filius noster Henricus, Rex Angliae et haeres Franciae."

FRANCE.　Nor this I have not, brother, so denied
But your request shall make me let it pass.

KING H.　I pray you then, in love and dear alliance,　325
Let that one article rank with the rest,
And thereupon give me your daughter.

FRANCE.　Take her, fair son, and from her blood raise up
Issue to me, that the contending kingdoms
Of France and England, whose very shores <u>look pale</u>　330
With envy of each other's happiness,
May cease their hatred; and this <u>dear conjunction</u>
Plant <u>neighbourhood</u> and Christianlike accord
In their sweet bosoms, <u>that never war advance</u>
His bleeding sword 'twixt England and fair France.　335

LORDS.　Amen!

KING H.　Now, welcome, Kate; and bear me witness all
That here I kiss her as my sovereign queen.　*Flourish.*

QUEEN.　<u>God, the best maker of all marriages,</u>
Combine your hearts in one, your realms in one!　340
As man and wife, being two, are one in love,

---

315 *According . . . natures* exactly as they were defined in the terms proposed [K].
316 *Where* whereas.　318 *for matter of grant* in official deeds conferring titles to land, etc.　319 *addition* title.　321 *Praeclarissimus* most illustrious. This should be "praecarissimus" "very dear" (like the French "très-cher"). Shakespeare copied a misprint in Holinshed without taking the trouble to correct it [K]. Holinshed had, in turn, carried over the error from Hall.　330 *look pale* i.e. because of the white cliffs on both sides of the Channel.　332 *dear conjunction* solemn union.　333 *neighbourhood* friendly feelings.　334 *that never war advance* in order that war may never lift up. "Advance" in this sense is common [K].　339 *God . . . marriages* According to the proverb "Marriages are made in heaven" [K].　342

So be there 'twixt your kingdoms such a <u>spousal</u>
That never may <u>ill office</u>, or <u>fell</u> jealousy,
Which troubles oft the bed of blessed marriage,
Thrust in between the <u>paction</u> of these kingdoms   345
To make divorce of their incorporate league;
That English may as French, French Englishmen,
Receive each other! God speak this Amen!

ALL.   Amen!

KING H.   Prepare we for our marriage; on which day,   350
My Lord of Burgundy, we'll take your oath,
And all the peers', for surety of our leagues.
Then shall I swear to Kate, and you to me,
And may our oaths well kept and prosp'rous be!

Sennet. Exeunt.

◆◆◆◆◆◆◆◆◆◆◆◆◆◆◆

[EPILOGUE]

Enter Chorus.

Thus far, with rough and all-unable pen,
   Our <u>bending</u> author hath pursu'd the story,
In little <u>room</u> confining mighty men,
   <u>Mangling by starts the full course of their glory.</u>
<u>Small time;</u> but in that small, most greatly lived   5
   This Star of England. Fortune made his sword;
By which the world's best garden he <u>achieved</u>,
   And of it left his son imperial lord.
Henry the Sixth, in <u>infant bands</u> crown'd King
   Of France and England, did this king succeed;   10
<u>Whose state so many had the managing</u>

---

spousal marriage.   343 *ill office* unfriendly acts.   *fell* cruel.   345 *paction* compact, agreement (THEOBALD; F¹: "Pation").

EPILOGUE The chorus speaks a regular Shakespearean sonnet.   2 *bending* bending over his desk; or, better, bending under the weight of the subject [K]; or perhaps "bowing."   3 *room* space.   4 *Mangling . . . their glory* depicting their glorious careers in disconnected fragments — as it were, by fits and starts [K].   5 *Small time* Henry's reign was rather brief.   7 *achieved* won.   9 *infant bands* swaddling clothes.   11 *Whose state . . . managing* During the childhood of King Henry VI, England was ruled by his uncles, who spent much of their time quarrelling among themselves.

That they lost France and made his England bleed;
Which oft our stage hath shown; and for their sake
In your fair minds let this acceptance take.   [*Exit.*]

---

13 *Which oft our stage hath shown* An allusion to the popularity of the three
parts of KING HENRY VI [K]. *for their sake* for the sake of those plays [K].   14
let this acceptance take let this play meet with your approval.